THE CHILD
AND THE
DAY CARE
SETTING

THE CHILD
AND THE
DAY CARE
SETTING

QUALITATIVE VARIATIONS
AND DEVELOPMENT

EDITED BY
RICARDO C. AINSLIE

PRAEGER SPECIAL STUDIES • PRAEGER SCIENTIFIC

New York • Philadelphia • Eastbourne, UK
Toronto • Hong Kong • Tokyo • Sydney

Library of Congress Cataloging in Publication Data

Main entry under title:

The child and the day care setting.

    Bibliography: p.
    Includes index.
    1. Day care centers--Addresses, essays, lectures.
2. Child development--Addresses, essays, lectures.
3. Parent and child--Addresses, essays, lectures.
I. Ainslie, Ricardo C.
HV851.Q33   1984   362.7'12   84-6836
ISBN 0-03-070291-7 (alk. paper)

I wish to thank Julie Rubin for her assistance in preparing the index for this volume.

**Published and Distributed by the
Praeger Publishers Division
(ISBN Prefix 0-275)
of Greenwood Press, Inc.,
Westport, Connecticut**

Published in 1984 by Praeger Publishers
CBS Educational and Professional Publishing,
a Division of CBS Inc.
521 Fifth Avenue, New York, NY 10175 USA

456789 052 9876545321

Printed in the United States of America
on acid-free paper

To Chris Anderson, a beloved friend and colleague, who contributed immensely to my development in the all too brief time we knew one another. And to Chris's family, Jim and Meaghan Anderson.

Preface

This volume contains contributions to the understanding of day care as a diversified, complex developmental setting. Collectively, they undermine the traditional assumptions among researchers that day care settings are readily comparable, and that variations within and between settings need play only a minor role in how we understand this increasingly important social institution. Instead, what is fleshed out in this volume is a multilayered perspective of day care environments. The contributors both document these diverse characteristics empirically and discuss their implications with a view toward enhancing our conceptual understanding of the day care situation and its implications for child development.

Day care as a social institution has developed rapidly. Whereas in the early seventies, when researchers began studying day care, substitute care was an unusual occurrence, today it is rapidly becoming the norm. In the last decade the number of young children in some form of substitute care has continuously increased so that presently well over a third of all children under the age of three are in substitute care. With some notable exceptions, efforts to understand the implications of day care for the development of children have not kept apace with these changes. In the first chapter of this volume, Jay Belsky creates the context for the entire collection by focusing on the central question of the second wave of day care research: Under what conditions do children fare best in day care? Belsky's chapter also provides us with an historical perspective within which we can understand the development of day care as an increasingly ubiquitous fact of life and the simultaneous transformation of the questions which researchers in this area must attempt to answer.

Researchers have often tended to treat day care as a unitary experience, as if differences between day care settings were negligible. Similarly, elements within each setting which might substantially alter the nature of a child's experience were often glossed over. Yet, those familiar with day care settings know that what constitutes "day care" for any particular child is subject to considerable variation, even within the same room. Alison Clarke-Stewart and Christian Gruber's chapter brings this diversity into sharp relief. Their study examines a broad range of day care settings. While focusing on four major groups of child care arrangements, the multiplicity of features along which each of these arrangements can vary is substantial. Their chapter makes it clear that the complexity inherent in day care means that there is no uniform day care experience for children or their families.

Many factors that contribute to the structure of the day care experience do not even originate in the day care setting, and therefore are difficult to appreciate if one approaches day care as if it could be studied independently from the rest of the child's world. For example, parents of children in day care vary considerably in their feelings about placing their children in substitute care. The sources of these different attitudes probably manifest themselves in a variety of ways in the parent-child relationship, all of which may affect the manner in which a child experiences being in day care. The chapter by Mark Everson, Lela Sarnat, and Sueann Ambron illustrates some of the ways in which maternal attitudes seem to affect the day care child.

Children in day care also develop different kinds of relationships with their caregivers. Caregivers, being human, often prefer some of their charges over others. Similarly, a variety of factors affect the child's feelings toward the caregiver. Further, in some day care settings there may be a variety of caregivers with whom each child has a substantially different relationship. Two chapters examine the nature of the child's relationship to the caregiver in some detail. The chapter by Ricardo Ainslie and Christine Anderson presents a theoretical framework within which the conditions which might facilitate infant-caregiver attachment are explored. This chapter also compares the quality of childrens' relationships to their mothers and caregivers. Similarly, the chapter by Dale Farran, Margaret Burchinal, Susan East Hutaff, and Craig Ramey examines in considerable detail the development of infants' relationships to their caregivers over time, drawing extensively from day care observations.

Finally, the fact that day care constitutes an ongoing separation of the child from his or her primary caretaker has traditionally been the focus of concern for those interested in assessing the effects of day care on socioemotional development. The transition to day care is not uncommonly stressful for children. Arrival at the center constitutes an intersection of the child's two primary developmental contexts: home and day care. The last two chapters in this volume bring the issue of separation distress into sharp relief, each from a different perspective.

The chapter by Mark Cummings and Jessica Beagles-Ross focuses on the child's experience of separation distress as mediated by various characteristics of the infant-caregiver relationship. Ellen Hock's chapter approaches this same issue from the vantage point of the mother's separation anxiety; namely, how such anxiety is likely to play an important role in the child's reaction to separation from her. Thus, we learn from these two chapters just how complex children's separation distress is; and that this behavior, so frequently witnessed in the day care setting, is strongly influenced by factors within the setting as well as those manifestly external to it.

Together, the contributions which comprise this volume are an important step in the second wave of day care research. The contributors help us see both the variety of factors which are active within the day care setting, and the multiple ways in which these can affect a child's experience. To be sure, this is not an exhaustive examination of day care. Researchers are only beginning to do justice to the complexity of day care as a developmental context. However, the present efforts illustrate the extent to which we must relinquish narrow conceptualizations of component parts of a child's developmental situation as isolated and unidirectional in their effects. A perspective which emphasizes the interdependence of the important factors in the child's environment is of primary importance if we are to adequately understand a developmental context such as day care, and if we are to contribute to such settings in the direction of optimizing the experience of children who grow up within them.

Ricardo C. Ainslie
Austin, Texas

Contents

List of Contributors

RICARDO C. AINSLIE
Educational Psychology Department
University of Texas at Austin
Austin, TX

SUEANN R. AMBRON
Educational Software at Human Engineered Software
San Francisco, CA

CHRISTINE W. ANDERSON
Educational Psychology Department
University of Texas at Austin
Austin, TX

JESSICA BEAGLES-ROSS
Pitzer College
Clairmont, CA

JAY BELSKY
Department of Individual and Family Studies
Pennsylvania State University
University Park, PA

MARGARET BURCHINAL
Department of Psychology
University of North Carolina at Chapel Hill
Chapel Hill, NC

ALISON CLARKE-STEWART
Program in Social Ecology
University of California at Irvine
Irvine, CA

E. MARK CUMMINGS
Laboratory of Developmental Psychology
National Institute of Mental Health
Bethesda, MD

MARK D. EVERSON
Division for Disorders of Development and Learning
University of North Carolina at Chapel Hill
Chapel Hill, NC

DALE C. FARRAN
Frank Porter Graham Child Development Center
University of North Carolina at Chapel Hill
Chapel Hill, NC

CHRISTIAN P. GRUBER
College of Education
University of Chicago
Chicago, IL

ELLEN HOCK
Department of Family Relations and Human Development
and Department of Pediatrics
Ohio State University
Columbus, OH

SUSAN EAST HUTAFF
Charlotte-Mecklinburg School System
Charlotte-Mecklinburg, NC

CRAIG T. RAMEY
Frank Porter Graham Child Development Center
University of North Carolina at Chapel Hill
Chapel Hill, NC

LELA SARNAT
Children's Health Council
Palo Alto, CA

1.

Two Waves of Day Care Research: Developmental Effects and Conditions of Quality

Jay Belsky

The effects of day care on children's development has been a concern of parents, scientists, and policymakers for quite some time. The traditional strategy for rearing children, especially within the middle-class, was, until the 1970s, for mothers to remain in the home and rear their offspring on their own, at least for the first five years. Demographic statistics bearing on the labor force participation of women reveal most strikingly how much things have changed during the past 10 to 15 years. It should be noted, however, that while this increase in female employment has been most marked during the last decade and a half, it represents a trend that has continued since World War II.

Between 1940 and 1975 the number of women participating in the labor force doubled (Hill, 1977, 1978), and by 1980 more than one-half of all women were working. This dramatic change in American economic and family life has been most pronounced for women with children, with the number of working mothers increasing eight-fold between 1940 and 1975 (Hill, 1977, 1978). Whereas only 18 percent of mothers with children under six years of age were employed outside the home in 1955 (Office of the Assistant for Planning and Evaluation, HDEW, 1974), ten years later the figure was 20 percent and, in 1977, 41 percent (Hofferth, 1979). By 1980, those mothers with children six to 17 years old were the most likely to be working, with 64 percent in the labor force. But even for women with young children, labor force participation has been increasing. In fact, 42 percent of women with children under three were working in 1980 (Waite, 1981). Projections reveal that this rate of growth will continue to produce an estimated six million working mothers

1

with children under six by 1985—a 32 percent increase over a
brief 10 year period (Hill, 1978). Indeed, it is estimated that
by 1990 three out of every four mothers will work (Urban Institute, 1980).

One major consequence for children of the increasing numbers of women entering the labor force, either for reasons of
personal fulfillment or economic need, is that they are being
cared for by persons other than their parents. Until recently,
such nonparental care was viewed as a necessary evil, to be
employed by the working poor or to be called upon in times of
national emergency (e.g., World War II industrial mobilization).
But as the women's movement has gained increased acceptance,
and as economic pressures, including inflation, unemployment,
and high interest rates, have made middle-class lifestyles all
the more difficult to achieve and maintain, the utilization and
acceptance of day care has grown.

Such increased reliance upon nonmaternal, supplementary
child care has had the effect of altering both scientific concerns
for, and public attitudes toward, day care. As noted above,
day care was initially regarded as a necessary evil for children
whose parents had to work—that is, women needed in the factories
during World War II and impoverished women who needed to
support their families. But as more and more families have come
to rely upon some form of day care, the minority status of day
care users has changed. This, in and of itself, would likely
have altered attitudes toward day care and changed the focus
of research and policy. But also influential have been the scientific data that have been generated regarding the effects of
day care on child development.

These two forces of influence on scientific and popular
regard for day care reveal what might be regarded as two waves
of concern and inquiry regarding day care. It is these two
waves of the scientific investigation of day care that are the
focus of this chapter. In the first wave, the principal issue
was whether day care was bad for children. Prevailing cultural
attitudes, many of which were influenced by scientific theory
and research, contended that exclusive maternal rearing, particularly during the early years, was essential to healthy psychological development. This resulted in the principal organizing
question of day care research being "Does rearing outside of
the confines of the family in a group program adversely affect
intellectual, social and, especially, emotional development?"
It should be clear that this specific interest in the developmental
consequences of day care, and particularly a concern for negative
effects, derived from policymakers' and scientists' obligation to

protect the public from harm. If day care proved detrimental
to development, it would be hard to make a case that it was in
the public's best interest and, as a consequence, that policies
should be adopted to promote, or even support, the group rearing of young children beyond the confines of the family. Of
course, if such early rearing experience was found to disrupt
the normative course of early childhood, mothers would be
obliged not to work unless it was absolutely essential.

It will be argued in this chapter that the results of the
first wave of research revealed few, if any, inevitable deleterious
consequences of day care rearing. As a result, a second wave
of research was initiated. This addressed the issue, "Under
what conditions do children fair best in day care? That is,
what types of rearing environments prove most supportive of
children's development?" In recent years, it is this second
issue that has become the principle concern of policy-minded
child developmentalists studying day care. Presumably, if
conditions of care that promote optimal development can be
identified, then a policy imperative would exist to encourage
such conditions. At the very least, there would exist an obligation to assure that inadequate conditions of care not be tolerated,
especially if purchased with tax revenues.

THE FIRST WAVE: THE DEVELOPMENTAL EFFECTS
OF DAY CARE

Research on the effects of day care can be usefully organized
around three topics—intellectual, emotional, and social development (Belsky and Steinberg, 1978; Belsky, Steinberg, and
Walker, 1982). Before proceeding to present such a review,
it is necessary to highlight once again the very real limits of
research designs for studying the effects of day care. Up until
the past five years, most inquiry into day care was restricted
to university-connected centers providing high quality care
(e.g., Ricciuti, 1974; Ramey and Campbell, 1979a and 1979b;
Kagan, Kearsley, and Zelazo, 1978). More than ever, however,
social scientists are moving beyond highly controlled settings
to investigate the nature and effects of community sponsored
day care (e.g., Blanchard and Main, 1979; Golden et al., 1978;
Rubenstein and Howes, 1979; this volume). This new work
tells us not simply what the effects of day care can be for
children fortunate enough to be enrolled in special programs,
but what they are likely to be for the overwhelming majority
of children in day care who are not exposed to programs with

special educational curriculums, well-trained staff, and good caregiver-child ratios.

An even more serious concern from the standpoint of design than sample limitations are the potential pre-existing differences that characterize children reared in day care and at home. In most investigations of the effects of day care, two samples are compared, one using day care, the other being reared at home. Such comparative designs are founded upon the assumption that where developmental differences exist they can be attributed to variation in child care experience. But a major problem, perhaps the major problem, of such designs, and indeed the "Achilles' heel' of day care research, is that important differences are likely to characterize home reared and day care reared comparison groups before variation in child care is experienced (Roopnarine and Lamb, 1978). Under such circumstances the attribution of subsequent developmental differences to day care, and thus the very notion of day care effects, may be inappropriate.

This brief analysis of two of the major limits in day care research could easily and understandably lead the rigorous scientist to the conclusion that research on the effects of day care cannot be done well, or at least not well enough so that it is useful for drawing valid conclusions. There are two reasons why one should not draw this conclusion. The first is that if the principal question is whether day care is bad for children, then even nonperfectly controlled designs can answer this question. Unless we presume that families which place their children in day care do a better job of caring for their offspring before and during their placement, then comparisons which consistently reveal few differences between day care- and home-reared children should allay most fears that parents, scientists, and policymakers are likely to have. Thus, while research designs might not be the best possible to document the effects of day care per se, they appear to be good enough to chronicle deficits that may be associated with (as opposed to caused by) day care rearing.

The second cause for confidence in available day care research derives from the data themselves. Despite limits in design and especially measurement, findings across studies are surprisingly consistent, even if not perfectly uniform. And, as I hope to show, even where inconsistency is markedly apparent, this too appears both explainable and meaningful.

INTELLECTUAL DEVELOPMENT

Ever since the Soviet Union beat the United States into space with the launching of Sputnik in the 1950s, Americans have displayed great concern for the intellectual development of their children. In point of fact, this is one reason why the theories of Piaget and the cognitive perspective in general have come to dominate the American psychological scene over the past two decades. Concern for the effects of day care on intellectual functioning merely reflects this historical influence.

An overwhelming majority of studies of the effects of day care on subsequent intellectual development have indicated no differences between day care-reared children and matched home-reared controls (Belsky, Steinberg, and Walker, 1982). Although a number of these investigators had found initial gains in one or many test subscales, all significant differences between day care children and matched controls disappeared during the program or soon after termination. In the only long-term follow-up study in this area, 102 of 120 Swedish children initially investigated by Cochran (1977) during infancy were found at 5-1/2 years of age to be equal in intelligence regardless of whether they had been continuously reared in a day care center, family day care home, or in their own homes by their parents (Gunnarson, 1978). For children from relatively advantaged families, then, exposure to day care, even to high quality, cognitively enriched programs, does not appear to result in any long-term gains in IQ test performance. Neither, though, does it seem that any losses in intellectual performance result from enrollment in day care.

In contrast to this conclusion regarding children from advantaged families, it is of significance that positive effects of the day care experience on performance on standardized tests of intellectual development have been reported by a handful of investigators for those children who have been categorized as higher risk than the average middle-class child. It should be noted, however, that most of the programs in which these economically-disadvantaged children were enrolled were specifically designed to provide cognitive enrichment, although they varied widely in the type and degree of special enrichment provided for the children and families involved (Belsky and Steinberg, 1978). Lally (1973), for example, found that while 29 percent of a low education, home-reared group obtained an IQ below 90 on the Stanford-Binet test, only 7 percent of a day care group did so. On the basis of these results, it would appear that an enriching day care experience may reduce some of the adverse effects typically associated with high-risk environments.

Further support for this conclusion comes from a longitudinal study of day care-rearing beginning in early infancy (Ramey, Dorval, and Baker-Ward, 1981). In this work, three groups of children were compared: (1) a high-risk experimental group enrolled in a specially designed cognitive enrichment day care program; (2) a high-risk, home-reared control group matched to the experimentals on a number of important variables (e.g., social class, age, sex, race); and (3) a general population contrast group reared at home in more economically advantaged households. During the period between six and 18 months, performance on the mental developmental subscale of the Bayley Infant Test declined for the high-risk controls (from 104 to 86), while it remained stable (near 104) for the high-risk experimentals (who were <u>randomly</u> assigned to the day care-rearing group). In addition, motor development subscale scores on this same test revealed significant differences between these two groups, favoring the day care-reared children.

Follow-up comparisons demonstrate that these patterns of decline in the level of functioning for the home-reared, economically disadvantaged children and of stability for their day care-reared counterparts continue into the child's third, fourth, and fifth years of life. In fact, while only 11 percent of the day care-reared children are scoring in the range of cognitive-educational handicap (i.e., IQ $\leq$ 85) at age five, a full 35 percent of the home-reared controls are scoring below this level of functioning. A possible reason for this difference is suggested by a recent analysis by O'Connell and Farran (1982) of these children's linguistic functioning when observed with their mother at 20 months during free play and a structured give-and-take-an-object session. The experimental children cared for in day care since their opening months of life engaged in more spontaneous showing of objects, and relied upon words more frequently when giving and requesting. In sum, they appeared more linguistically and communicatively competent, and it is just such competency upon which subsequent intellectual growth is likely to build.

The overall picture of evidence, duly qualified, suggests that the day care experience has neither beneficial nor adverse effects on the intellectual development (as measured by standardized tests) of most children. For economically disadvantaged children, however, day care may have an enduring positive effect, for it appears that such day care experience may <u>reduce the declines in test scores</u> typically associated with high-risk populations after 18 months of age (Belsky and Steinberg, 1978; Belsky, Steinberg, and Walker, 1982).

Emotional Development

Historically, the mother-child bond has been of prime concern to those interested in the influence of early experience upon emotional development. Psychoanalytic theory and early research on institutionalized children (e.g., Bowlby, 1951; Spitz, 1945) suggested that any arrangement which deprived the child of continuous access to its mother would impair the development of a strong maternal attachment and thereby adversely affect the child's emotional security. Since day care, by its very nature, entails the daily separation of mother from child, a good deal of attention has been devoted to discovering whether child care outside the home does indeed disrupt the child's emotional tie to his mother. The major strategy for making such an appraisal has been to observe young children's responses to separation from and reunion with their mothers (usually in an unfamiliar laboratory playroom), and to see whether children prefer to interact with their mothers, their caregivers, or a stranger in free play situations.

In a very early, and therefore noteworthy study, Blehar (1974) observed disturbances in the attachment relationships that children, 30 and 40 months of age, and enrolled in day care for five months, had developed with their mothers. Specifically, while the 30 month-old children were more likely to show "anxious-avoidant" attachments to their mothers (more resistance and avoidance behavior and less proximity seeking during reunion) than were their home-reared counterparts, the 40 month-old children manifested "anxious-ambivalent" attachments (less exploration prior to separation, more crying and searching during separation, and more proximity seeking and resistance behavior to mother during reunion). In each age group, the home-reared comparison subjects were more likely to greet their mothers positively following the stressful separation experience, a behavioral style that is considered to index a secure emotional attachment (Sroufe, 1979). Much criticism has been levelled against this study (Belsky and Steinberg, 1978), and an attempt to replicate Blehar's 40-month results, using many more methodological controls, failed to find the home care/day care differences she discerned (Moskowitz, Schwarz, and Corsini, 1977).

Results from several other investigations are contradictory in showing that either day care- (Cochran, 1977; Ricciuti, 1974)

or home-reared children (Doyle and Somers, 1977) are more
likely to get distressed upon separation from the caregiver.
It seems ill advised, however, to interpret group differences
on a single measure as indicative of a meaningful and functionally
significant difference in psychological development (Belsky and
Steinberg, 1978). This would seem especially true in the case
of a measure of distress following separation from mother, since
Kagan and his colleagues (1978) have observed that distress to
separation shows virtually the same developmental course in
children reared in markedly different contexts around the world,
suggesting that it may be more maturationally programmed than
experientially influenced. This is probably the reason why
Kagan et al. (1978) found, in the most comprehensive and controlled study to date, that at between 3-1/2 and 30 months of
age, day care- and home-reared infants did not differ in their
emotional responses to a separation from mother.

Further evidence of similar patterns of emotional development in day care- and home-reared children comes from a series
of studies of 10-12 month-olds (Brookhart and Hock, 1976),
5-30 month-olds (Doyle, 1975), 36 month-olds (Roopnarine and
Lamb, 1978), and 41-45 month-olds (Portnoy and Simmons, 1978).
In each investigation, response to a separation from and reunion
with mother were generally equivalent between groups that
varied in early rearing experience. Why then do Blehar's (1974)
previous results differ so markedly? Two explanations come to
mind—one historical, the other developmental.

It is important to note that Blehar's children were enrolled
in day care in the early 1970s, at a time when day care, especially for very young children, was still looked upon negatively
by many people. Possibly, then, the guilt that parents may
have experienced in violating cultural standards, or even the
quality of care that was offered when day care was such a
relatively new phenomenon, could have adversely influenced
the Blehar subjects. Thus, a cohort effect, emphasizing the
historical timing of day care enrollment, might be responsible
for her divergent results.

Additionally, it needs to be noted that Blehar's children
were only in day care for five months when evaluated. Recent
evidence indicates that a "transient distress reaction" may be
associated with initial adaptation to daily separation from parents
and thus may account for Blehar's data. Support for this
possibility comes from several sources. First, Portnoy and
Simmons (1978), who first proposed this explanation, were
unable to replicate Blehar's results, but studied children who
averaged 9-1/2 months of day care experience prior to assess-

ment. And, in an entirely independent study, Blanchard and Main (1979) found that avoidance of mother, both during daily pick-up from day care and in a structured laboratory situation, decreased the longer the child had been in day care. These findings suggest, then, that young children may go through a period of stressful adaptation to supplementary child care. But once they come to understand that regular separation from parent need not imply loss of the attachment figure, adaptation is achieved and problematic behavior is reduced.

It is important to emphasize that beyond the just discussed transient-distress reaction, negative effects of day care may be absent primarily when supplementary child care arrangements are reasonably stable and care is of a reasonable quality. In fact, a recent study of infants enrolled prior to their first birthday in unstable (i.e., frequently changing) day care arrangements reveals that children in such poor quality care arrangements are at risk for developing anxious-avoidant attachment relations with their mothers (Vaughn, Gove, and Egeland, 1980). An unrelated investigation by Schwartz (1984) also indicates that infants starting full-time day care placement during the first year display more avoidance of their mothers when reunited with them following a brief separation at 18 months. Attachment relations characterized by high levels of such avoidance, and thus classified as insecure, have been found to predict problems in adjusting to peers during the preschool years (Arend, Gove, and Sroufe, 1979).

A follow-up study of the children in the Vaughn et al. (1980) investigation led its authors to conclude that even these apparently negative effects may not be long lasting: "at two years of age the effects of out of home care were no longer striking. . . . For this sample, then, it appears that the cumulative adverse effects of out-of-home care were minimal" (Farber and Egeland, 1982, p. 120). Despite these conclusions, it should be noted that several trends were apparent in Farber and Egeland's data on children's behavior during a problem-solving episode which could lead a more cautious reader to a different conclusion. Specifically, toddlers whose mothers began working prior to their infants' first birthday displayed significantly less enthusiasm in confronting a challenging task than children who had had no day care experience. Furthermore, they tended to be less compliant in following their mothers' instructions and were less persistent in dealing with a difficult problem than children who had never been in day care or who began day care after their first birthday. Finally, they, like the late-entry day care children, tended to display more negative affect.

In a recent and provocative reanalysis of the Farber and
Egeland (1982) data, Vaughn, Deane, and Waters (1984) demonstrate that the effects of early day care entry are indeed long
lasting, "but can only be understood when the interaction of
attachment history and nonmaternal care experiences are considered together" (p. 37, ms). For children classified as
anxiously attached to their mothers at 18 months of age, no
effect of day care emerged; such children, regardless of day
care utilization or timing of entry into day care continued to
display less competent and more maladaptive behavior in the
problem solving situation at 24 months. For children evaluated
as securely attached at 18 months, however, those who had
entered day care before one year of age received "substantially
less optimal scores on the 24-month measures than their home
care counterparts" (p. 37, ms). Indeed, although children
who were secure at 18 months and whose mothers never worked
looked more competent at two years than the insecure children
from the early work group, no differences in functioning in
the problem-solving task were evident between children who
were secure at 18 months and whose mothers started work
before 12 months and insecure children whose mothers never
worked.

Since the initial Vaughn et al. (1980) analysis indicated
that early entry is associated with greater anxious-avoidant
attachments, and since these new data indicate that limits in
child functioning become evident by two years of age even when
the attachment history was characterized by security, there
seems to be cause for concern about early entry into the kind
of routine day care that is available in most communities. This
would seem to be especially true in view of two additional recent
studies which also raise questions about early entry into day
care. In one which was conducted in Bermuda, and will be
discussed in more detail when we consider the second wave of
day care research, McCartney and her colleagues (1982, p. 148)
found that "children who began group care in infancy were
rated as more maladjusted (when studied between three and
five years of age) than those who were cared for by sitters
or in family day care homes for the early years and who began
group care at later ages." These conclusions, it is important
to note, were based upon analyses which controlled for a variety
of important background variables, including child's age at time
of assessment and mother's IQ, age, and ethnicity. In a retrospective investigation of eight to 10 year olds who had varied
in their preschool experiences, Barton and Schwarz (1981)
also found day care entry prior to 12 months of age to be asso-

ciated with higher levels of misbehavior and greater social withdrawal, even after controlling for the education of both parents.

These new data lead one to modify conclusions that have been arrived at in past reviews in order to underscore the potentially problematical nature of early entry into community-based, as opposed to university-based, day care (Belsky and Steinberg, 1978; Belsky, Steinberg, and Walker, 1982). Supplementary child care exerts little influence on the child's emotional ties to his/her mother (other than transient distress) except under certain conditions, as when children are enrolled in unstable or poor quality day care arrangements prior to their first birthday. Under such conditions, infants may be more likely to develop a particular kind of disturbance in their relations with their primary attachment figure: They will be likely to avoid her. Further, they may be more likely to display emotional and social problems in subsequent years. Important to note, though, is the fact that such deleterious consequences may not be long-lasting or inevitable. Recall that Farber and Egeland themselves concluded that little effect of early entry was evident at two years. Further, studies of high quality care have failed to discern negative consequences of early entry (Ricciuti, 1974; Kagan, Kearsley, and Zelazo, 1978; Ramey, Dorval, and Baker-Ward, 1981).

Social Development

Earlier it was noted that both economics and ideology play a major role in the utilization of day care in the United States, as increasing numbers of mothers with young children are working outside the home—either for reasons of financial necessity or personal fulfillment. To fully understand such early reliance on group rearing, one also needs to recognize the value that American culture places on independence. In marked contrast to the Japanese, for example, who view their newborns as independent and thus in great need of developing dependency relations with parents, family, and community, Americans view the newborn as exceedingly dependent, needing to be weaned from his excessive reliance on others if he is to succeed in a society as competitive and individualistic as the United States (Caudill and Weinstein, 1969; Kagan et al., 1978). Thus, it should be of little surprise that one important reason American families place their children in group rearing situations is to give them the opportunity to be independent of their families and to learn how to get along with others, most especially their peers. When it comes to assessing the effects of day care on social development, then, primary attention has been directed toward children's behavior toward peers and nonparental adults.

With respect to peer relations, available evidence indicates that day care has both positive and negative effects. On the positive side, Ricciuti (1974) and Kagan et al. (1978) have shown that one- to two-year olds with group experience during infancy are more willing to approach a strange peer or continue their play in the presence of an unfamiliar agemate, and Clarke-Stewart (1979) has reported that two- and three-year olds cared for in day care centers, nursery schools, or family day care homes display more cooperation while playing with a strange peer and are better able to appraise the perspective of another than are agemates reared by their mother or a babysitter at home. More recently, Vliestra (1981) has reported, on the basis of observations of two and a half- to four and a half-year olds, that those experiencing full-day care, in contrast to those experiencing half-day care (for at least six months), engaged in significantly more positive interaction with peers and displayed more of what she regarded as prosocial aggression (tattling, defending property against counterattack, commanding, enforcing rules), but not more hostile aggression (physical or verbal attack on others). Studies such as these and others (Gunnarson, 1978) clearly suggest that day care rearing may enhance certain social competencies, probably by providing children with early and increased opportunities to relate to peers. That these effects may be enduring is suggested by Moore's (1975) study of adolescents: Boys who had experienced group rearing prior to the age of five reported higher concern for social activities and were also observed to be more sociable with peers and found to be chosen more regularly by peers as likable than were boys who were home reared during their preschool years.

On the negative side, Moore (1964) observed that when these children were preschoolers, those in supplementary child care arrangements (which were often unstable) were more prone to toilet lapses and were more self-assertive. Schwarz et al. (1974) found, in one of the first studies to raise concerns about the effect of day care, that preschoolers with day care experience in infancy were more aggressive (both physically and verbally) toward peers than a group of home-reared children who were enrolled in day care for the first time when three to four years old. Vliestra's (1981) earlier mentioned study raises some questions, however, about these results, which were based upon observer ratings. While her observational data comparing children with part-time and full-time exposure to day care failed to demonstrate that full-time care was associated with greater aggression, teacher ratings indicated that the full-time children were more aggressive. This contradiction, she suggests, may be a result of the greater activity levels of the full-time children which could have been interpreted as aggression by teachers. The relevance of this interpretation for the Schwarz et al. (1974) study is to be found in the fact that this early investigation discerned greater activity on the part of preschoolers with extensive day care experience. Could it be that aggression and activity were also confused in the Schwarz study?

While this possibility cannot be discounted, the situation is further confused by a recent retrospective study by Barton and Schwarz (1981) who compared the teacher and peer ratings of 191 eight- to ten-year olds from white middle-class families who varied in day care exposure during their preschool years. After controlling for maternal and paternal education, analyses revealed no differences on teacher ratings of children, but peer ratings indicated that full-time day care exposure was associated with more aggression and attention getting—what Barton and Schwarz referred to as misbehavior. Although the evidence is by no means totally consistent, it does repeatedly suggest that in some respects day care children engage in more negative interactions with peers. Another reading of these data is that with greater peer exposure comes greater peer interaction, which is more likely to be both positive and negative in quality.

When it comes to relations with adults, and the socialization of adult-like behaviors, the available evidence also raises concerns. In the initial Schwarz et al. (1974) investigation, observations and teacher reports revealed that preschoolers with extensive day care experience were less cooperative with adults, more physically and verbally aggressive toward them, and somewhat less tolerant of frustration. Results consistent with these data were reported a decade earlier by Raph et al. (1964) who found that negative interactions between middle- and upper-class first graders and their teachers varied directly with the amount of group-rearing the children experienced prior to first grade. Paralleling these results are recent findings from a retrospective analysis of five- and six-year olds who were reared at home or in day care during the preschool period. Robertson (1982) observed that boys with day care histories were rated by their teachers as substantially and significantly more troublesome than peers cared for at home. Specifically, these day care-reared boys were more likely to be rated as

having little respect for other children and as being quarrel-
some, disobedient, and uncooperative. Consistent with these
findings are those reported as part of a retrospective study of
two-year olds from Bermuda who had been cared for in day
care centers, by babysitters, or by mothers during their first
years of life. Analyses which included statistical controls for
variation in maternal and paternal IQ, education, and occupation
indicated that, in testing situations with adults, center-reared
children were more apathetic, less attentive, and less socially
responsive (Schwarz et al. 1981).

Additional evidence also suggests that day care-reared
children may orient to peers more than to adults. Schwarz et al.
(1974) found, for example, that while preschoolers with prior
day care experience interacted more with peers than teachers,
the opposite was true of the home-reared children who were
having their first group experience at age three to four (Lay
and Meyer, 1973). Similar results have been reported by
McCutcheon and Calhoun (1976) who observed that increased
interaction with peers was accompanied by decreased interaction
with adults in day care. The implications of this trend are
suggested by several results from Moore's (1964) initial study
that indicate that day care-reared preschoolers are less conform-
ing and less impressed by punishment.

Given these potentially disturbing effects of day care on
social development, several comments are in order. Lest these
data be taken as a sweeping indictment of day care rearing, it
must be noted that

> . . . like all social and educational efforts, day care
> programs are likely to reflect, and in some measure
> achieve, the values held explicitly or implicitly by
> their sponsors and, through them, by the community
> at large.
>
> From this perspective, the tendency we have
> observed for all-day group care to predispose chil-
> dren toward greater aggressiveness, impulsivity,
> and egocentricism may represent a phenomenon
> specific to American society, for these outcomes
> have been identified as characteristic of socializa-
> tion in age-segregated peer groups in America
> generally. . . . That the phenomena may indeed
> be culturebound is indicated by . . . comparative
> studies of peer group socialization in the United
> States, the USSR, Israel, and other contemporary
> societies, which show that, depending on the goals

and methods involved, group upbringing can lead
to a variety of consequences, ranging from delin-
quency and violence at one extreme to unquestion-
ing conformity at the other (Belsky and Steinberg,
1978, p. 942).

Ambron's (1980) recent suggestion that day care staff
are more permissive, more tolerant of disobedience and aggression, and less inclined to set behavior standards than parents
is consistent with these conclusions. So too is McCrae and
Herbert-Jackson's (1975) claim that the effects of day care may
be program specific. Empirical support for these speculations
can be found in Gunnarson's (1978) Swedish day care study,
the findings of which contradict much of the data reviewed
above. Specifically, naturalistic observations of five-year olds
reared since infancy in day care centers, family day care homes,
or in their own homes, revealed no rearing-group differences
in children's compliance and cooperation with, and positive
affect expressed towards, adults. Moreover, structured doll
play assessments of these five-year olds revealed that day
care children were no more likely than home-reared children
to transgress against adult wishes in the face of peer pressures
to do so. However, children reared in Swedish day care centers, in comparison to those reared in homes (by family day
care providers or mothers), did engage more frequently in
information sharing, compliance, and cooperation with peers.
These data demonstrate not only that day care can promote
positive peer skills, but that negative interactions with peers
and adults which have been reported regularly enough so that
they cannot be disregarded, need not be more frequent in any
rearing environment. This leads us to reaffirm the conclusion
quoted earlier: The effect of day care on social development
will likely depend on the community and cultural context in
which day care is employed as well as the particular practices
of the day care program.

Summary

The findings with respect to cognitive development are
probably the most easy to summarize. There is no evidence
that day care influences the intellectual functioning of children
other than those from impoverished homes who are reared in
centers during infancy. Exactly how long such supplementary
child care experience buffers these children from the intellectual

declines so frequently observed among their home-reared counterparts remains to be seen. With respect to emotional development, available evidence generally fails to support the notion that supplementary child care negatively affects the child. Indeed, new evidence suggests that many of the negative effects that have been found for day care vis-a-vis infant-mother attachment may be more a function of the timing of assessment than supplementary care per se. After six months of day care experience, young children seem to successfully adapt to their supplementary care arrangements so that they are virtually indistinguishable from their home-reared counterparts. Where group differences are evident, little consistency across studies can be found, suggesting that the discerned effects of day care rearing are program specific or unreliable.

These conclusions seem to hold true except under circumstances in which children are enrolled in care that is not of high quality prior to their first birthday. Such early enrollment has been associated with the development of anxious-avoidant attachment (Vaughn et al., 1980) and later maladjustment (McCartney et al., 1982; Barton and Schwarz, 1981). In view of the many failures to discern a similar effect when children are reared in high quality programs, it cannot be emphasized enough that these conclusions pertain to the potentially deleterious consequences of early experience in poor quality care. What this suggests, of course, is that very early day care experience need not be problematic. Under conditions of high quality, development, at least so far as has been studied to date, need not be compromised.

With respect to social development the news is both good and bad. Exposure to day care seems to increase both positive and negative interactions with agemates; further, there is repeated evidence that this form of childrearing may also make children less oriented and responsive to adult socialization. Since such findings are by no means replicated in all or even most studies, either in this nation or in others, it cannot be concluded that these are necessary consequences of day care. Indeed, the failure to discern negative effects in many studies clearly suggests that while such disturbing consequences can be produced by day care rearing, they need not be.

This point is extremely important from the standpoint of policy. In response to the science- and policy-oriented question, "Is day care bad for children?", it seems appropriate to conclude that it usually is not and certainly does not have to be, but that it can be. In view of this conclusion, the orientation of scientists and policymakers is forced to shift from one of day care

effects to the conditions of care that produce different consequences. This would seem to be especially so since parents
who work need child care of some sort. If some arrangement
must be made, it would seem to be incumbent upon a society
to know what are the best conditions for such care or, at the
very least, what are the conditions to be avoided. Fortunately,
day care research by child developmentalists has responded
to this shift in focus; indeed, it may have even preceded it.

THE SECOND WAVE: CONDITIONS OF QUALITY

Research designed to evaluate the effects of day care
routinely involves the comparison of children whose experiences
have varied markedly. Some have been reared in day care,
others by their own parents. Such between-group designs
afford scientists and policymakers little insight into those
contextual conditions which are most supportive of development.
Indeed, such inference is possible only indirectly—by comparing
the results of investigations which sampled children from different day care rearing milieus. Such between-study comparisons
are inherently problematical because of the large number of
factors across which investigations vary in addition to the
quality of programs from which they have sampled children.
Indeed, given the diversity of methods, procedures, and ages
of subjects, study by study comparisons are only useful at the
most global level of analysis, like a comparison of the results
of investigations which relied upon community-based programs
and those which relied upon university-sponsored, research-
oriented programs to examine the effects of day care. In the
preceding analysis, reference was made to just such global
comparisons.

The limits inherent to such approaches are the same as
those inherent to social class comparisons. Although one may
be able to document that class is related to some developmental
outcome, the question of how or why remains empirically un-
answerable because of the lack of specificity in the construct
of social class. Recognition of this limit has led researchers to
examine variation within a social class in order to determine
how a set of experiences which may be probabilistically associated with a particular socioeconomic niche influences development.

A comparable awareness has led policy-minded students
of child development to examine variation within day care milieus
in recent years. In part this work has been motivated by the

recognized limits of home care versus day care comparisons.
It is also motivated, however, by the realization that day care
is here to stay and thus that policymakers need to know about
the conditions of day care, especially those that can be regulated,
and how they affect the child's development. Toward this end,
three approaches to specifying quality have been undertaken.
One set of studies examines how regulateable dimensions of
day care, what will be referred to as social structural parameters
of day care, relate to child development. Investigations falling
within this set attempt to relate dimensions of day care such as
group size, caregiver-child ratio, caregiver training, and
whether or not a family day care home is licensed or regulated
directly to the child's intellectual, emotional, and/or cognitive
development.

From a scientific standpoint such studies are limited since
they cannot specify why or how such social structural parameters
influence the child. In recognition of this weakness, a second
set of studies attempts to link social structure with experience,
since social structure is presumed to directly influence the
types of experiences children actually have on a day-to-day
basis in day care. But why is this important? Because it is
assumed that it is experience that influences development. In
other words, this second set of investigations represent an
effort to identify the experiential consequences of social structure.

But these investigations, too, are limited, since they
rarely include an assessment of the child's development. Thus,
although variation in group size or caregiver training is linked
to variation in experience, experience is rarely linked to development. And this, of course, is the weakness that the third set
of studies addresses. Specifically, these investigations make
an effort to relate observed variation in experience, scaled on
a high-to-low quality basis, to developmental outcome.

Because only a single study has tried to coordinate all
three pieces of this causal model (social structure → experience →
development), it is most useful to discuss these investigations
in blocks, weaving together results in order to generate a
coherent picture. This is what will be done in this section in
order to document what is currently known about the conditions
and consequences of quality care.

Social Structure and Child Development

Group size, caregiver-child ratio, and caregiver training
are the dimensions of day care which have received the most

systematic attention by investigators interested in learning how
parameters of day care available to legislative regulation influence, or at least covary with, individual differences in the
development of children reared in day care. The National Day
Care Study, which involved the systematic investigation of 67
day care centers in three major metropolitan areas (Atlanta,
Detroit, and Seattle), was specifically designed to address
issues of concern to policymakers. Consequently, sites and
centers were chosen to maximize the diversity of the sample;
centers varied widely in staff characteristics, staff-child ratios,
group sizes, and in the per-child expenditures and ethnic and
socioeconomic composition of client populations (Ruopp and
Travers, 1982).

Analyses of the performance of approximately 1,000 children
on standardized tests of cognitive and linguistic development at
two times of measurement (fall and spring) revealed that group
size and caregiver training were the most important determinants
of variation in children's development. Specifically, children
cared for in small groups showed significantly greater improve-
ment across testing periods on examinations designed to measure
kindergarten and first grade reading readiness. Further, the
specialized training of caregivers in subject areas pertinent to
child care was also positively associated with child achievement.

Size of day care group has also been implicated in a recent
study of the care received by 64 two-year olds in Bermuda who
had experienced family day care or center care during their
first two years (Schwarz et al., 1981). In this investigation,
maternal reports indicated that the size of the day care rearing
group which children experienced during their first and second
year of life was negatively associated with a variety of developmental outcomes assessed when children were two years of age.
Specifically, large group experiences during the first year were
found to predict poor coordination, limited verbal expressive-
ness, and behavioral deviancy. Similar experience during the
second year of life was related to limited attention span as well
as poor coordination at the 24 month testing. While the influence
of a poor caregiver-child ratio also appeared to be problematic,
its pernicious effect seemed most striking when group size was
also considered. Children who were reared in large programs
with few adults per child displayed low attention spans, behavioral deviancy, hyperactivity, and an introverted style.

Stability of care is another dimension of social structure
which merits consideration in any attempt to discern the processes
by which variation in care influences child development. Unfortunately, and surprisingly, very little work exists on this

important topic. Rubenstein and Howes's (1979) study of experiences at home and in day care suggests that in addition to the
frequent claim that a low turnover rate among staff is in the
child's best interest, so too is a stable peer group. Stability
has also been implicated as an important dimension of quality
care in Cummings' (1980) investigation of emotional functioning.
Observations made during separation from the mother during
daily morning drop-offs at day care revealed that toddlers
were more likely to become upset when left with a caregiver
identified as unstable than when left with one with whom the
child was very familiar. Finally, the earlier-reviewed Vaughn
et al. (1980) findings regarding the detrimental effect of day
care on attachment when supplementary care is initiated in the
first year and tends to be unstable also underscore the importance
of this dimension of the day care experience.

Having found that certain parameters of the social structure
of day care environments are systematically related to how children fair in day care, there is cause to wonder why such results
obtain. Evidence which addresses this issue is reviewed next
by considering research linking social structure with variation
in experience.

Social Structure and Daily Experience

If parameters of day care structure like size, ratio, and
caregiver training are predictive of the effect that day care
will have on a child, it is probably because aspects of day care
determine, at least in part, the nature of the child's daily
experiences in care. To what extent is there evidence to sub-
stantiate this claim that the social structure of day care is
associated with the experiences children have? To answer
this question, we turn first to analyses of group size and ratio.

Center/group size and child-caregiver ratio are the characteristics of centers that have received the most empirical attention in efforts to understand how variations in programs affect
children's experience. In an early observational study of 69
California preschool/day care programs, Prescott, Jones, and
Kritchevsky (1967) found that when center population exceeded
60, more emphasis was placed upon rules and routine guidance
than when size ranged from 30 to 60 children. Teachers, in
fact, placed twice as much emphasis on control in the large
groups, possibly accounting for the observation that in small
centers children displayed more pleasure, wonder, and delight.
Additional evidence from this study revealed that large centers

were less flexible in their scheduling, offered children fewer opportunities to initiate and control activities, and had teachers who displayed less sensitivity to the individual needs of the children (Heinicke ct al., 1973).

Recently, most of these findings have been replicated in the National Day Care Study. Ruopp and Travers (1978) reported that for children three to five years of age, group size was the single most important determinant of the quality of children's experience. In groups of less than 15 to 18 children, caregivers were involved in more embellished caregiving (e.g., questioning, responding, praising, comforting), less straight monitoring of children, and less interaction with other adults. And in these smaller groups, children were more actively involved in classroom activities, like considering and contemplating, contributing ideas, cooperating, and persisting at tasks. On the basis of these findings, and others to be reviewed shortly, it seems reasonable to draw the conclusion that size affects caregiving, which in turn influences child functioning in day care. This may well be the reason why size is also associated with day care outcomes.

Interestingly, the NDC study found that the child-to-caregiver ratio had little effect upon the quality of preschoolers' experience in day care, though it was an important determinant of infants' experiences. More overt distress was observed among children under three as the number of children per caregiver increased. Additionally, in such high ratio infant and toddler programs, staff spent more time in management and control interactions, and engaged in less informal teaching (Connell, Layzer, and Goodson, 1979; Ruopp and Travers, 1978). Biemiller, Avis, and Lindsay (1976) reported similar findings in a small study comparing two infant day care programs.

Other investigations also underscore group size and ratio as important determinants of the quality of children's experience. As part of an investigation of 40 toddlers in 16 day care homes and eight day care centers, Howes (in press) carried out systematic observations (each lasting two hours) on 20 caregiver-toddler dyads in each of these types of day care settings. Results revealed that caregivers with fewer children in their care (low group size, low ratio), who worked shorter hours, and who had less housework responsibilities, engaged in more facilitative social stimulation (talk, play, demonstrate, toy, touch), expressed more positive affect, were more responsive, and less restrictive and negative. More years experience as a child care worker and more formal training in child care were also related to the provision of such "high quality" care, it should be noted.

In another investigation by Howes, 55 middle-class toddlers
from 11 day care centers and 16 family day care homes were
observed (Howes and Rubenstein, 1981). Toddlers in both
settings with ratios of three or fewer children per caregiver
engaged in more responsive and spontaneous talking and were
more positively affective, as revealed by high levels of laughing,
smiling, and sharing than those in settings with between three
and a half and six children per caregiver. This observed difference in child behavior was quite possibly a function of the fact
that, in those locales with higher ratios, caregivers engaged
in more spontaneous talking, more hugging and holding, and
more social mediation of objects.

Given the pattern of findings that seems to be emerging,
it should not be surprising that Vandell and Powers (1982)
reported similar results in their observational investigation of
55 white, middle-class preschoolers (ages 3 to 5) at six different
centers varying in quality. High quality centers, operated by
universities, were characterized by a low caregiver-child ratio
(1:5), high levels of teacher training and child care experience,
large amounts of space per child, and many toys, whereas low
quality centers had high ratios (1:24), low levels of teacher
training and experience, and less adequate toys. Sixteen
minutes of observation on each child revealed that, in the high
quality centers, children were more likely to interact positively
with adults, and less likely to engage in solitary activities or
to be uninvolved in any sustained activity.

Several of the studies mentioned above included analyses
of family day care homes as well as day care centers. Beyond
parameters like size, ratio, and caregiver training, it should
be noted that three different types of family day care homes
can be distinguished. Unregulated homes are those that are
not licensed or registered by a public agency. Unregulated
care, although illegal in many cases, is the most prevalent
form of family day care. Indeed, a 1971 survey estimated that
unlicensed care constituted 90 percent of all day care arrangements (Westinghouse/Westat, 1971). In regulated or licensed
care, the provider has been licensed by a state, county, or
local government agency (e.g., department of human resources,
county board of health). Across the nation there is considerable
variation in licensing standards, but most deal with group composition (i.e., staff-child ratio) and basic health and safety
measures. Licensed homes are visited (often irregularly) by
local officials who review the health and safety of the environment. Finally, sponsored or supervised homes are part of networks or organizations of child care providers. These are

groups of licensed caregivers whose organization provides them
with referrals and training or other child support services
(e.g., play material). Such networks frequently work on the
assumption that provision of training and assistance to caregivers improves the quality of care provided.

A recent study of 41 sponsored (i.e., supervised), 35
licensed, and 23 unlicensed family day care (FDC) homes tends
to corroborate this assumption. On the basis of lengthy,
naturalistic observations, Hawkins and her colleagues (Hawkins
et al., 1979; Carew, 1979) found that sponsored caregivers
were most involved with their children (e.g., teaching, helping,
offering direction), while providers in unlicensed homes were
least involved. Moreover, these sponsored homes were found to
offer safer physical environments (Stallings & Porter, 1980).
Probably as a consequence of such differences between types
of family day care, toddlers in the unlicensed homes were more
likely to spend time on their own, not interacting with anyone;
were most frequently unhappy; and were most inclined to
engage in antisocial behavior (Carew, 1979). Such differences
in caregiving environments and children's experiences in family
day care are probably a function, at least in part, of the fact
that unlicensed homes tend to have less favorable adult-child
ratios than do licensed and supervised homes (Emlen, 1977;
Hall and Weiner, 1977).

On the basis of the work reviewed in this section, we see
that those aspects of the social structure of day care which
have been related to the developmental consequences of day
care tend also to covary in a meaningful manner with variation
in day-to-day experiences in day care. Such a pattern of
covariation provides support for the assumption that size, ratio,
and training influence child development by shaping experience.
In order to make the strongest case possible for this inference,
we turn next to investigations linking variation in day-to-day
experience to variation in the effects of day care.

Daily Experience and Child Development

Studies that speak to the issue of how experience in day
care influences the development of children exposed to such
rearing have assessed a variety of outcomes which can be
broadly distinguished in terms of those that assess socioemotional
development and those that focus upon cognitive-linguistic
development. Interestingly, there exists striking similarity
across studies in the dimensions of experience that have been

sampled, even though measurement procedures vary from caregiver or maternal reports to systematic behavioral observation.
The fact, too, that results are strikingly consistent makes these
studies relatively easy to summarize. In this section, then, a
relatively global summary will be offered of five different
investigations before focusing in detail upon the single most
comprehensive study of this issue to date.

Golden and his colleagues (1978) studied approximately
400 children reared at home or enrolled in one of 31 service-
oriented, licensed, public and private, community controlled,
group and family infant day care programs in New York City.
Carefully collected observational assessments of the physical
and social caregiving environments at 12, 18, and 24 months
revealed that two-year olds who experienced high levels of
cognitive and social stimulation scored appreciably higher on
measures of social competence and language comprehension when
they were three.

Complementing these findings are those from another
large scale investigation of infant-toddler day care, this one
conducted in California. Kermoian (1980) found, on the basis
of observations of more than 225 infants in various child care
arrangements, that those in low quality milieus—characterized
by infrequent play and instructional interactions with caregivers, and frequent negative interactions, were less sensitive
to experimental mother-infant separations than were those reared
in high quality centers. The infants' failure to get distressed
during separation or to reduce their exploratory activity suggested to the investigator that low quality care may increase
the development of avoidant attachment relations.

Variation in day care experience appears to affect the
quality of the child's emotional tie to its caregiver as well as
to its parent. Such a conclusion emerged from an investigation
assessing the effect of variation in physical environment and
caregiver involvedness of 17 day care centers serving 35 white,
middle-class children ranging in age from 19 to 42 months
(Anderson et al., 1981). Children observed in the strange
situation who come from centers where caregivers were observed
to interact frequently with the children and where planned
daily routines and activities, attractive physical space, and age-
appropriate equipment characterized the centers, behaved in a
way suggestive of a secure relationship to their caregivers.
Specifically, the children exposed to such care explored more
freely and showed a preference for interacting with the familiar
caregiver over the stranger. In contrast, children from centers
of low physical quality and/or low caregiver involvedness dis-

played a preference for interacting with the stranger whom they had never before encountered.

Rubenstein, Howes, and Boyle's (1979) small scale study of infant day care also highlights the importance of caregiver involvement—a theme that keeps reappearing in these analyses linking variation in day-to-day experience to variation in child functioning. In their follow-up study of ten three and a half year olds cared for in centers since 12 months of age, they reported that frequency of social play with caregiver predicted subsequent greeting behavior upon reunion with mothers ($r = .70$) in a separation situation, while caregiver directiveness (i.e., intrusiveness) predicted future temper tantrums ($r = .67$). The possibility is raised in this study that these day care experiences which appeared to influence later development may have been instigated by the children themselves; for example, infants who were more socially oriented tended to elicit more playful interaction from their caregivers.

The developmental significance of the quantity and quality of caregiver involvement is most apparent in a comprehensive investigation of 156 families with preschoolers in day care centers on the island of Bermuda (McCartney et al., 1982). The subjects of this study, it is of interest to note, ranged in age from 36 to 60 months and represented virtually the entire population of preschoolers in day care on the island. Observations of children and interviews with directors were utilized to gather information on the activities children were exposed to and the stimulation they encountered. Child functioning was assessed using standardized assessments of language, social, and emotional development, and data were gathered on family background so that hierarchical multiple regression analyses could be carried out controlling for confounding factors. The first variables entered into regression equations to predict child functioning were characteristics of children's families, including child age, and maternal IQ, education, and ethnicity. In the next step, status characteristics of group care were entered, including age at entry and the mean number of hours the child was in care. Finally, indices of the quality of care experience were entered; these included measures of the frequency with which the child was spoken to by an adult when alone and when a part of a group, and an overall quality of environment score based upon over 50 questions from two instruments completed by specially trained raters after extended observations of each center.

Results revealed, consistent with findings reported already, that even after controlling for background characteristics, variation in quality significantly predicted linguistic and social

competence. Specifically, a measure of adaptive language and
two ratings of intelligence and task orientation were strongly
affected by variation in quality among centers. In fact, in the
case of language, nearly 20 percent of the variance was accounted
for by differences in quality. With respect to social development,
nearly half the variance in sociability (i.e., extroversion) from
a standardized measure of classroom behavior (filled out by
parents and teachers) was accounted for by total quality;
similarly a measure of consideration for others was also predicted
by positive aspects of the day care milieu. In contrast, children
rated as dependent tended to come from centers with low overall
quality. Furthermore, poor emotional adjustment (i.e., anxious,
hyperactive, or aggressive behavior), as rated by caregivers,
tended to occur in centers with low levels of adult verbal interaction with children.

In sum, "children at the better quality centers score higher
on measures of language development. . . . Caregivers at
higher quality centers note their children as more sociable and
considerate than do caregivers with centers with less adult-child
verbal interaction and poorer overall quality" (McCartney et al.,
1982, p. 147). Centers with limited verbal interaction also have
children who look less emotionally well adjusted, as revealed by
higher levels of anxiety hostility/aggression, and hyperactivity.

CONCLUSION

On the basis of the preceding analyses, it should be clear
that not all day care is the same. There exists great variation
in the social structure, experience, and the outcomes associated
with day care exposure. Further, on the basis of the data
reviewed, a case can be made for the claim that social structure
influences experience, which in turn affects child development.
As we have seen, in centers and family day care homes in which
group size is modest, ratios are low and staff training is high,
caregivers tend to be more stimulating, responsive, and positively
affectionage, as well as less restrictive. Moreover, children
who experience such care tend to be more cooperative, more
intellectually capable, and more emotionally secure.

What is so especially intriguing about these results of
investigations aimed at chronicling the conditions of quality
day care is how consistent they are with research on family
influences on child development. Whether we look at the research
on infancy or early childhood (for reviews see Belsky, Lerner,
and Spanier, 1984; Clarke-Stewart, 1977), there is consistent

evidence that certain qualities of parental care promote optimal psychological development. In infancy we speak of mothers being sensitive to their children, and during the preschool years Baumrind's (1967) notion of the authoritative (as opposed to the permissive or authoritarian) parent captures the essence of quality care. Operationally these terms refer to parents who are involved with their children, responsive to their needs and controlling of their behavior, but not too restrictive. Such growth facilitating care also relies heavily upon linguistic communication, which we know fosters general intellectual development, as well as the use of inductive as opposed to power-assertive discipline, which we know fosters prosocial development. It would seem that in quality day care, that is, in care systems in which physical and personal resources are not overextended, sensitive, authoritative care is also provided, and in this setting it continues to facilitate human development.

What this analysis suggests is that it is not where the child is reared that is of principal importance but how he or she is cared for. One's social address does not determine development, be it home care, day care, lower-class, middle-class. Rather, it is the day-to-day experiences one has which shapes psychological growth. Social structure is influential because it probabilistically influences whether certain experiences will be experienced. When group size is large and ratios are poor, individual attention to children falls victim to the exigencies of coping with an overextended set of resources. Either restrictions and controlling behavior increase, or disregard and aimless behavior on the part of the child increases. Neither is in the child's best interest. But when the necessary human resources are available, daily experiences tend to be stimulating and rewarding, and child development is facilitated. This is as true in a day care milieu as it is in a family environment.

REFERENCES

Ambron, S. Causal models in early education research. In S. Kilmer (Ed.), Advances in early education and day care, Vol. II. Greenwich, CT: JAI Press, 1980.

Anderson, C. W., Nagle, R. J., Roberts, W. A., and Smith, J. W. Attachment to substitute caregivers as a function of center quality and caregiver involvement. Child Development, 1981, 52, 53-61.

Arend, R., Gove, F., and Sroufe, L. A. Continuity of individual adaptation from infancy to kindergarten: A predictive study of ego-resiliency and curiosity in preschoolers. Child Development, 1979, 50, 950-959.

Barton, M., and Schwarz, C. Day care in the middle-class: Effects in elementary school. Paper presented at the American Psychological Association Annual Convention, Los Angeles, August 1981.

Baumrind, D. Child care practices anteceding three patterns of preschool behavior. Genetic Psychology Monographs, 1967, 75, 43-88.

Belsky, J., and Steinberg, L. The effects of day care: A critical review. Child Development, 1978, 49, 929-949.

Belsky, J., Steinberg, L., and Walker, A. The ecology of day care. In M. E. Lamb (Ed.), Nontraditional families: Parenting and child development. Hillsdale, NJ: Erlbaum, 1982.

Belsky, J., Lerner, R., and Spanier, G. The child in the family. Reading, MA: Addison-Wesley, 1984.

Biemiller, A., Avis, C., and Lindsay, A. Competence supporting aspects of day care environments—a preliminary study. Paper presented at the Canadian Psychological Association Convention, Toronto, June 1976.

Blanchard, M., and Main, M. Avoidance of the attachment figure and social-emotional adjustment in day care infants. Developmental Psychology, 1979, 15, 445-446.

Blehar, M. Anxious attachment and defensive reactions associated with day care. Child Development, 1974, 45, 683-692.

Bowlby, J. Maternal care and mental health. Geneva, Switzerland: World Health Organization, 1951.

Brookhart, J., and Hock, E. The effects of experimental context and experiential background on infants' behavior toward their mothers and a stranger. Child Development, 1976, 47, 333-340.

Carew, J. Observation study of caregivers and children in
    day care homes: Preliminary results from home observations.
    Paper presented at Biennial Meetings of the Society of
    Research in Child Development, San Francisco, April 1979.

Caudell, W., and Weinstein, H. Maternal care and infant be-
    havior in Japan and America. Psychiatry, 1969, 12, 32-43.

Clarke-Stewart, A. Child care in the family. New York, NY:
    Academic Press, 1977.

Clarke-Stewart, A. Assessing social development. Paper
    presented at the Biennial Meeting of the Society for Research
    in Child Development, San Francisco, March 1979.

Clarke-Stewart, K. A. Observation and experiment: Complement
    any strategies for studying day care and social development.
    In S. Kilmer (Ed.), Advances in early education and day
    care. Greenwich, CT: JAI Press, 1980.

Cochran, M. A comparison of group day care and family child-
    rearing patterns in Sweden. Child Development, 1977, 48,
    702-707.

Connell, D. B., Layzer, J. I., and Goodson, D. National study
    of day care centers for infants: Findings and implications.
    Cambridge, MA: ABT Associates, unpublished manuscript,
    1979.

Cummings, E. M. Caregiver stability and day care. Develop-
    mental Psychology, 1980, 16, 31-37.

Doyle, A. Infant Development in Daycare. Developmental
    Psychology, 1975, 11, 655-656.

Doyle, A., and Somers, K. The effects of group and family
    day care on infant attachment behaviors. Canadian Journal
    of Behavioral Science, 1978, 10, 38-45.

Emlen, A. Family day care for children under three. Paper
    presented for the International Symposium on the Ecology
    of Care and Education of Children Under Three, February
    1977.

Farber, E. A., and Egeland, B. Developmental consequences
    of out-of-home care for infants in a low-income population.

In E. Zigler and E. W. Gordon (Eds.), Day care: Scientific and social policy issues. Boston, MA: Auburn House, 1982.

Golden, M. et al. The New York City Infant Day Care Study: A comparative study of licensed group and family day care programs and the effects of these programs on children and their families. New York, NY: Medical and Health Research Association of New York City, Inc., 1978.

Gunnarson, L. Children in day care and family care in Sweden: A follow-up. Bulletin No. 21, Department of Educational Research, University of Gothenburg, Sweden, 1978.

Hall, A., and Weiner, S. The supply of day care services in Denver and Seattle. Menlo Park, CA: Stanford Research Institute, Center for the Study of Welfare Policy, 1977.

Hawkins, P., Wilcox, M., Gillis, G., Porter, A., and Carew, J. Observation study of caregivers and children in day care homes. Paper presented at the biennial meeting for the Society of Research in Child Development, San Francisco, March 1979.

Heinicke, C., Friedman, D., Prescott, E., Puncel, C., and Sale, J. The organization of day care: Considerations relating to the mental health of child and family. American Journal of Orthopsychiatry, 1973, 43, 8-22.

Hill, C. R. The child care market: A review of evidence and implications for federal policy. In Policy Issues in Day Care: Summaries of 21 Papers. Washington, D.C., Department of Health, Education, and Welfare, 1977.

Hill, C. R. Private demand for child care: Implications for public policy. Evaluation Quarterly, 1978, 2, 523-545.

Hofferth, S. Day care in the next decade: 1980-1990. Journal of Marriage and the Family, 1979, 644-658.

Howes, C., and Rubenstein, J. L. Determinants of toddler experience in daycare: Social-affective style age of entry and quality of setting. Unpublished manuscript, University of California, Los Angeles, 1981.

Howes, C. Caregiver Behavior and Condition of Caregiving. Journal of Applied Developmental Psychology. In Press.

Kagan, J., Kearsley, R., and Zelazo, P. Infancy: Its place in human development. Cambridge, MA: Harvard University Press, 1978.

Kermoian, R. Type and quality of care: Mediating factors in the effects of day care on infant responses to brief separation. Paper presented at the International Conference on Infant Studies, New Haven, CT, May 1980.

Lally, R. The family development research program: Progress report. Unpublished paper, Syracuse University, 1973.

Lay, M., and Meyer, W. Teacher/child behaviors in an open environment day care program. Syracuse University Children's Center, 1973.

Macrae, J. W., and Herbert-Jackson, E. Are behavioral effects of infant day care programs specific? Developmental Psychology, 1975, 12, 269-270.

McCartney, K., Scarr, S., Phillips, D., Grajek, S., and Schwartz, J. C. Environmental differences among day care centers and their effects on children's development. In E. Zigler and E. W. Gordon (Eds.), Day care: Scientific and social policy issues. Boston, MA: Auburn House, 1982.

McCutcheon, B., and Calhoun, K. Social and emotional adjustment of infants and toddlers in a day care setting. American Journal of Orthopsychiatry, 1976, 46, 104-108.

Moore, T. Children of full-time and part-time mothers. International Journal of Social Psychiatry, 1964, 2, 1-10.

Moore, T. Exclusive early mothering and it's alternatives: The outcome of adolescence. Scandinavian Journal of Psychology, 1975, 16, 255-272.

Moskowitz, D., Schwarz, J., and Corsini, D. Initiating day care at three years of age: Effects on attachment. Child Development, 1977, 48, 1271-1276.

O'Connell, J. C., and Farran, D. C. Effects of day-care experience on the use of intentional communicative behaviors in a sample of socioeconomically depressed infants. Developmental Psychology, 1982, 18, 22-29.

Office of the Assistant for Planning and Evaluation. The
    Appropriateness of the Federal Interagency Day Care
    Requirements (FIDCR): Reports on Findings and Recommenda-
    tions. Washington, D.C.: United States Department of
    Health, Education, and Welfare, June 1974.

Portnoy, F., and Simmons, C. Day care and attachment.
    Child Development, 1978, 49, 239-242.

Prescott, E., Jones, E., and Kritchevsky, S. Group day care
    as a child rearing environment. Final report to Children's
    Bureau. Pasadena, CA: Pacific Oaks College, 1967.

Ramey, C. T., and Campbell, F. A. Compensatory education
    for disadvantaged children. School Review, 1979, 87, 171-
    189. (a)

Ramey, C. T., and Campbell, F. A. Early childhood education
    for psychosocially disadvantaged children: The effects of
    psychological processes. American Journal of Mental Defi-
    ciency, 1979, 83, 645-648. (b)

Ramey, C., Dorval, B., and Baker-Ward, L. Group day care
    and socially disadvantaged families: Effects on the child
    and the family. In S. Kilmer (Ed.), Advances in early
    education and day care. Greenwich, CT: JAI Press, 1981.

Raph, J., Thomas, A., Chess, S., and Korn, S. The influence
    of nursery school on social interaction. Journal of Ortho-
    psychiatry, 1964, 38, 144-152.

Ricciuti, H. Fear and development of social attachments in the
    first year of life. In M. Lewis and L. A. Rosenblum (Eds.),
    The origins of human behavior: Fear. New York, NY: Wiley,
    1974.

Robertson, A. Day care and children's responsiveness to
    adults. In E. Zigler and E. Gordon (Eds.), Day care:
    Scientific and social policy issues. Boston, MA: Auburn
    House, 1982.

Roopnarine, J., and Lamb, M. The effects of day care on
    attachment and exploratory behavior in a strange situation.
    Merrill-Palmer Quarterly, 1978, 24, 85-95.

Rubenstein, J. L., and Howes, C. Caregiving and infant be-
     havior in day care and in homes. Developmental Psychology,
     1979, 15, 1-24.

Rubenstein, J. L., Howes, C., and Boyle, P. A two year
     follow up of infants in community based infant day care.
     Paper presented at the biennial meeting of the Society for
     Research in Child Development, San Francisco, March 1979.

Ruopp, R., and Travers, J. Janus faces day care: Perspectives
     on quality and cost. In E. Zigler and E. W. Gordon (Eds.),
     Day care: Scientific and social policy issues. Boston, MA:
     Auburn House, 1982.

Schwarz, J. C., Scarr, S. W., Caparulo, B., Furrow, D.,
     McCartney, K., Billington, R., Phillips, D., and Hindy, C.
     Center, sitter, and home day care before age two: A report
     on the first Bermuda infant care study. Paper presented at
     the American Psychological Association, Annual convention
     in Los Angeles, August 1981.

Schwarz, J., Strickland, R., and Krolick, G. Infant day care:
     Behavioral effects at preschool age. Developmental Psy-
     chology, 1974, 10, 502-506.

Schwartz, T. Length of Day Care Attendance and Attachment
     Behavior in 18 month olds. Child Development. In Press.

Spitz, R. A. Hospitalism: An inquiry into the genesis of
     psychiatric conditions in early childhood. Psychoanalytic
     Study of the Child, 1945, 1, 53-74.

Sroufe, L. The coherence of individual development. American
     Psychologist, 1979, 34, 834-841.

Stallings, J., and Porter, A. National Day Care Home Study:
     Observation component. Draft final report to the Day Care
     Division, Administration for Children, Youth, and Families,
     Department of Health, Education, and Welfare, April 1980.

Urban Institute. The subtle revolution: Women at work.
     Washington, D.C.: The Urban Institute, 1980.

Vandell, D. L., and Powers, C. P. Day care quality and
     children's free play activities. Unpublished manuscript,
     1982.

Vaughn, B., Deane, K., and Waters, E. The impact of out-of-home care on child-mother attachment quality: Another look at some enduring questions. Invited Presentation to the Department of Pediatric Psychology, Rush University Medical School, Chicago, Ill., March 1983.

Vaughn, B., Gove, F., and Egeland, B. The relationship between out-of-home care and the quality of infant-mother attachment in an economically disadvantaged population. Child Development, 1980, 51, 1203-1214.

Vliestra, A. G. Full versus half-day preschool attendance: Effects in young children as assessed by teacher ratings and behavioral observations. Child Development, 1981, 52, 603-610.

Waite, L. U.S. women at work. Population Bulletin, 1981, 36(2).

Westinghouse Learning Corporation and Westat Research, Inc. Day care survey—1970: Summary report and basic analysis. Washington, D.C.: Office of Economic Opportunity, 1971.

2.

Day Care Forms and Features

K. Alison Clarke-Stewart
and Christian P. Gruber

Most research on day care contrasts the "traditional" at-home-with-mother care arrangement with one form of alternative care: the day care center. But the question this research was designed to answer—whether children in day care differ from their home-reared peers—is fast losing its relevance. For reasons of economic or psychological necessity approximately 40 percent of the mothers of preschool children in this country are already using some form of day care for their children. For parents in these families the important question about day care overlaps with that of child care professionals: how to provide the young child with the best possible day care environment. Their concern is with knowing which aspects of day care distinguish the programs in which children do well from those in which they suffer. Responding to this concern, the present chapter reports results from one study of the forms and features of day care environments as they were related to children's intellectual competence and social skills.

The research reported in this chapter was supported by the Bush Foundation, supplemented by funds from the Spencer Foundation. The assistance of these Foundations is most gratefully acknowledged. Appreciated, too, is the assistance provided by various graduate students at the University of Chicago who collected, coded, and helped in the analyses of data. Particularly helpful for this report were the efforts of Linda May Fitzgerald and Saba Ayman-Nolley.

When any parents choose a day care setting for their child they get a package of day care components. The woman who runs the day care home down the block is 37 years old, has been taking in children for the last eight years, and has three toddlers and an infant in her care this week. The university-based nursery school across town has three teachers with Montessori training, serves 25 children who are from two to four years old, boasts a well-equipped playyard, but closes for two months during the summer. The parents must make a choice between these two complex arrangements. They cannot transfer the special warmth they liked in the sitter's home to the nursery school, nor can they bring the more elaborate play equipment and staff of the nursery school to the day care home. Just realizing the complexity of such differences between settings may begin to confuse the parent making the decision. Yet these are but two possibilities. The parents might, in addition, inter-view a variety of sitters who would come into their home, and visit a number of day care centers that would offer them a wide range of full-day services. It was to get information that might help parents choose among the myriad of day care arrangements and programs possible, by finding out which aspects of day care settings were most likely to enhance or hinder children's development, that we conducted the Chicago Study of Child Care and Development.

As we tried to systematize the confusing conglomerate of day care alternatives, we identified two major sets of distinctions. One set comprised the distinctions between day care "forms" or "types." Preliminary field work surveying families in Chicago uncovered a plethora of child care forms in use. In fulfilling their own individual needs and desires families had created some highly specialized arrangements involving relatives, neighbors, paid sitters, and professional educators. Moreover, to cover idiosyncrasies in the parents' work schedules and the availability of day care services, these day care providers were frequently used in combination and often changed from one month to the next. During the summer a child might be at nursery school Monday and Wednesday mornings, with grandma Tuesdays and Thursdays afternoons and go to a neighbor's house on alternate Fridays. In the fall, he might spend full-time in a day care center. At a general level, however, there were just two types of care from which parents made their individual choices and created their unique arrangements: sitter care and center care. Within these general categories the distinctions between child's home and sitter's home and between nursery school and day care center represented two

major and meaningful variations. To investigate the significance
of distinctions among day care forms, therefore, we selected
for study the following four types of day care arrangements:
babysitters in the child's home, day care homes, nursery
schools, and day care centers. Calling on a number of sources
(including pediatricians, churches, and a purchased mailing
list from a book service intended for parents of young children),
we then located a sample of 80 2- and 3-year olds from families
in Chicago who were using one of these four arrangements and
who were willing to commit themselves to the demands of the
study.*

The other set of distinctions comprised the "features"
or "components" of particular day care settings—the number
of children, the quality of the physical environment, and the
characteristics of the caregiver. To tap variability in day
care features, we chose no more than four children from any
one setting. Altogether, 63 day care settings were represented
in the study. To get information about what went on in these
different day care settings, researchers interviewed each child's
parents and caretaker(s) at length and made systematic observations and ratings of the physical environment, the composition
of staff and child participants, and the activities in which the
children engaged in the day care setting. From these interviews
and observations we were able to put together brief descriptive
sketches characterizing the four day care forms in terms of
their typical features.

To assess the possible significance of differences in day
care forms and features, we also measured children's social
and intellectual competence three times over the period of a year.
These measurements were based on a number of standard structured and unstructured situations in which children were placed,

---

*Although a concerted effort was made to recruit approxi-
mately equal numbers of children of the same ages (2 and 3
years) for the four child care arrangements at the beginning
of the study, there ended up being more and older children in
center arrangements than in home arrangements (n = 47, mean
age = 39 months versus n = 34, mean age = 32 months). These
differences reflect real world phenomena: center attendance is
more likely for older preschool children, and parents using
centers were more accessible and willing to participate, and
had day care arrangements that fit our criteria more neatly.
Differences in number and age were controlled for statistically
in all analyses.

at home and in a laboratory playroom at the university. The
measures of developmental competence were then statistically
related to the form and features of the day care arrangements
of individual children.

This was a study of children in the "real world," but
there are limitations on how broadly our findings may be applied.
The sample we located tended to overrepresent families at higher
socioeconomic levels. This was partly because of restrictions
we imposed (we eliminated families living in neighborhoods into
which we felt we could not safely send graduate research
assistants at night), partly because of the nature of the sources
of names that were available to us, and partly, we must assume,
because of sample self-selection. Almost half our sample were
from professional-class families, while only a quarter were from
lower than middle-class families. This sample bias probably
also led us to study better-than-average day care arrangements.
Consequently, we do not claim to have conducted a comprehensive or even representative survey of existing day care environments. However, we were careful to include a range of families
and day care facilities of each type and our measures of day
care components did demonstrate considerable variability, making
it possible to measure differences within as well as between day
care forms.

FORMS OF DAY CARE

Sitter Care

In-Home Sitters

When day care is necessary, the form working parents
most often claim to prefer is to have an adult who comes into
the family's home and looks after the children there. U.S.
Department of Labor statistics suggest that this form of care
is used by about one-third of the working mothers of preschool
children. Often (nationally, over half the time), the in-home
babysitter is a relative, who may or may not be paid. In our
study, which included 16 children in this form of day care,
four of the sitters were unpaid relatives; the rest were paid
for their services. The "typical" sitter in the Chicago Study
was an older woman (44 percent were over 55 years; the mean
age was 47) with limited education and professional training.
She was unlikely to have had professional experience in any
child-related field, to have graduated from high school, or to
have studied child development or early childhood education.

Only one of the in-home sitters in our study had worked with children professionally; only two had gone to college or taken a course in child development. These personal characteristics of age, experience, education, and training are one clear way in which sitter care differs from center care.

Another, even more obvious, way in which the two forms of day care differ is in their physical settings. The physical environment of a home is most decidedly different from that of a school or center. For one thing, it is less "child oriented." In our study, homes were likely to have significantly more "adult oriented" decorative elements such as drapes, books, carpets, plants, musical instruments, television and stereo equipment (an average of 20 in homes versus 12 in centers), and to have significantly fewer types of toys and educational materials such as puzzles, stuffed toys, push-pull toys, balls, books, arts and crafts materials, instructional games, or a child's tape recorder (12 different types available in homes versus 19 available in centers). Our observers also noted an average of five dirty or messy features in homes—perhaps an overflowing ashtray, dirty dishes left out, a broken toy, a stained rug, and a patch of paint peeling from a living room wall—and an average of two places in the homes which could expose the child to a degree of real danger, like an unprotected stairway, accessible cleaning supplies or medicines, a paring knife left on the kitchen table, and so on. In centers, observers found, on the average, only two messy features and one danger-ous one, both significantly less frequent.

While this lack of child orientation in the physical setting is noteworthy, it should be recognized that, for in-home sitter arrangements, these observations reflect conditions in the child's own home. The materials and decor are supplied by the child's parents with little input from the sitter. The dishes left out may well have been from a rushed family breakfast be-fore the sitter arrived, and certainly the sitter had little to say about the presence of curtains, pictures, or the piano in the livingroom. In the physical features of the environment, thus, in-home sitter care, unlike center care, does not differ from the care ordinarily provided by parents.

The child is embedded in a social milieu as well as a physical environment, and this is another area in which sitter care and center care differ. In most homes we observed, the in-home sitter had primary responsibility for the children during much of the day, although the mother, father, or another adult was also often present during a portion of our observation period. During her time in the home the sitter was responsible for the

care of only one or two children. The adult-child ratio for
in-home sitter care was thus (averaging fewer than two children
to each adult) the highest observed in any form of day care we
studied, significantly higher than in centers or day care homes,
and offered the child the greatest opportunity for one-to-one
adult-child interaction.

On the other hand, in-home sitter care presented the least
varied opportunities for the child to interact with other children.
When there was more than one child present in the home, the
other child was either an infant or an agemate and was usually
a sibling. No sitters were looking after children more than a
year older than the child in the study. Nor did visits with
other children—at home, in the park, at a neighbor's—when
under the sitter's supervision greatly augment this limited peer
contact. Observers found that children with in-home sitters
interacted with an average of fewer than two other children,
during their morning and afternoon observations. The child's
opportunity for peer interaction with an in-home sitter was
limited, for the most part, to exchanges with one other young
and socially unskilled playmate whom the child would have been
able to play with anyway. Moreover, in the own-home care
arrangements both the other child and the sitter were most
likely to be from the child's own ethnic and social group, thus
offering no exposure to cultural diversity. These differences
in social opportunity clearly differentiate in-home sitter care
from other forms of day care.

The limited opportunities provided by sitter care were
apparent not only to outside observers but to the sitters themselves. We asked the caregivers to rate the care arrangement
for the wealth of experiences it afforded the children across
a number of categories: opportunities for the child to learn,
opportunities to interact with a variety of adults and peers;
opportunities to use educational materials; exposure to socialization training; and opportunities to receive love and affection.
The in-home sitters gave ratings that were significantly lower
than those given by center caregivers; on a 4-point scale (poor,
fair, good, excellent) the sitters' average rating of their own
settings was between poor and fair.

In terms of how children spent their time in the care
arrangement, our observers described home care as considerably
less "structured" than center care. There were significantly
fewer planned activities or clearly defined activity areas with
related routines, less reliance on by-the-clock scheduling, and
so on. In home settings, activities were more likely to be woven
around the normal loose routines of a household—infants needing

to be fed and changed, lunch prepared, toys periodically
collected from the living room and returned to the toy chest
in the bedroom, parents greeted on their return home at different times each day. With only one or two children and few real
deadlines (unlike "pick-up" and lunch times in a nursery
school), these sitters have little need to create the structural
support that routines and organized activities provide. Indeed
it is likely this "homey" informality and flexibility, combined
with a greater sense of their own control over the environment,
that makes this day-care arrangement attractive and reassuring
to parents.

Day Care Homes

In the second form of sitter care the child goes to the
sitter's house or "day care home" for supervision while mother
is at work. This form of care is used by approximately 35
percent of the employed mothers of preschool children in the
United States. In our study, 20 children (mean age = 32 months)
were in day care homes at the beginning of the study; 7 were
in day care homes at the end (one year later). On the average
they spent 7-1/2 hours a day in the day care home (range = 4
to 12 hours). The 25 women who ran these day care homes
were found to be significantly younger (average age 36 years)
than the in-home sitters. Like them, however, they were unlikely to have had professional experience in a child-related
field (only about 15 percent of these day care home providers
reported such experience). But they did have more education,
both generally (the typical day care home provider had graduated
from high school and taken some college-level courses) and
specifically in child care or child development (half had taken
at least one course and two had taken six or more courses).
Their level of education was still significantly below that of
center-based caregivers for all these categories, however.
Although it is common for home day care to be provided by a
relative (43 percent of the day care homes nationally), in our
study only one day care home provider was a relative; only
two were unpaid.

As we suggested earlier, homes are clearly differentiated
from centers according to features of their physical environments. In our observations, day care homes, like children's
own homes, had relatively many adult decorative elements
(mean = 18), relatively few different types of toys and educational materials (mean = 12), and an average of about five messy
or dirty features and two dangerous ones. The high degree
of similarity between the physical features of day care homes

and children's own homes is somewhat puzzling at first glance.
One might expect more child centeredness in a facility specifically
in the "business" of providing child care and supporting the
care of five children rather than one or two. Yet it very likely
reflects a real phenomenon: a day care home is fundamentally
a home, even when it is stretched to take in more children or
to provide a service for a fee. It functions as a home for the
family who lives there, and most day care home providers, even
those who are doing it for profit, strive to incorporate their
young charges into their own family's routines, rather than
making child care a career and their home an institution.

The social milieu provided by day care homes, however,
unlike the physical environment, was distinct, not only from
centers, but from sitter care in the child's own home. Like the
in-home sitter, the day care home sitter was usually the sole
caregiver responsible, but she was caring for a significantly
greater number of children. In the "average" day care home
in our study there were five children (range three to ten children) and our target child interacted with almost all of them
during the observation periods. Thus, the day care home provides significantly more opportunities for interaction with
different children than the own-home arrangement. Moreover,
the group of children in any day care home was likely to be
more heterogeneous in its race, ethnicity, and socioeconomic
level, than the group of children with any in-home sitter.
Despite this diversity of social partners, however, day care
homes were nearly as limited as own-home arrangements in the
level of social interaction they afforded. None of the day care
homes we observed had children more than a year older than
the target child, so children's encounters were, as in own-home
care, limited to those with children of equivalent or lesser social
skills.

Center Care

Nursery Schools

Over a million preschool children in the U.S. today attend
nursery school. These child-oriented, center-based programs
have grown in popularity since they began in the 1920s, so that
now middle-class parents consider it desirable to provide some
kind of supplementary nursery school experience for their 3 or
4 year old children—and over a third of them do so. In our
study 22 children (mean age = 40 months) attended part-time
nursery school programs at the beginning of the study; 39 were

in nursery school a year later. Their "average" teacher was a 37 year-old woman—the same age as the average day care home provider. The big difference between these teachers and sitters, was in their "professionalism." Not only were teachers currently employed in a professional child-caring capacity, over 70 percent of them had had previous professional experience in a child-related field such as nursing, teaching, or social work. Nursery school teachers were all college graduates and nearly all (over 90 percent) had at least some formal training in child development at college. Half of them had had fairly extensive training in child development (more than six university level courses). These women had been in their present childcare settings, on the average, for nearly four years, longer than caregivers in any other form of day care.

As we have already described, children in centers were exposed to strikingly different physical settings compared to children at home. There were fewer "homey" decorations like drapes, lamps, pictures, and ornaments, but a significantly greater variety of toys and educational materials and equipment. Despite the number of children present, our observers found things kept quite neat and well-organized in the nursery schools they visited, with only a couple of messy features per setting, such as a broken toy, soiled rug, or a litter of paper in the art corner. Moreover, classrooms did not have such common house-hazards as cellar stairs or kitchen cutlery, and we found an average of only one potentially hazardous feature per setting.

Equally striking were differences in the social milieu of centers and homes. Instead of being in the company of a single adult, the child in a center was exposed to a number of grown-ups. In all the nursery school classes we visited there were at least three adults. And instead of a handful of children, there was a large group of peers to play with. In our study the average nursery school class size was 18, and children were observed to interact, on the average, with 10 of their classmates during a two-hour period. The resulting adult-child ratio of about 1:6 implies that while these children were exposed to a greater diversity of adults, the opportunities for individual supervision and one-to-one interaction with any adult were more limited in center than in home care arrangements.

On the other hand, the available peer group gives center-care children more opportunities for social experiences with peers who are more varied and more advanced. In our study most nursery school children were in classes where the age range was less than 2 years, but in one-fifth of the classes

there were children who were more than a year older than our
target 2- and 3-year olds, offering them more socially mature
playmates and models. Nursery-school classmates and caregivers were also significantly more likely to include a heterogeneous mix of family backgrounds, in terms of race, ethnicity,
and socioeconomic status, offering the child more variety of
social experiences in this way too.

When caregivers themselves rated the quality of care they
provided in terms of its opportunities for children's learning,
education, socialization, and interaction, nursery-school teachers
rated their programs between good and excellent. In support
of these ratings, our observers found center-based programs
significantly more likely than sitter arrangements to have
scheduled activities, to have clearly defined areas with associated routines, and to follow a formal curriculum.

This last feature epitomizes the "institutional" distinction
between homes and schools. Only about 10 percent of the
nursery-school teachers we talked to said that they used no
formal curriculum. Another 30 percent of them described their
curriculum as "eclectic"; 22 percent said they provided a "traditional nursery-school" curriculum; 20 percent said their curriculum followed the principles of open education; 6 percent of the
programs were Piagetian in orientation; 10 percent were Montessori programs; and one program used Distar methods and materials. When we asked caregivers to review a list of common aims
and values often stressed by early childhood educators and to
endorse the four goals emphasized most in their own programs,
we discovered that such curricular identifications went beyond
mere labels. Espoused goals matched the generally accepted
views of different curricula. "Traditional nursery-school"
teachers more often emphasized the need for discipline and
management, teaching socialization, and providing the opportunity for playful interaction, and less often emphasized the
need for providing opportunities for learning and intellectual
stimulation. Montessori teachers more often endorsed the need
to provide opportunities for learning and intellectual stimulation
and downplayed the importance of opportunities for playful
interaction. Teachers in both Piagetian and open education
programs stressed the need to provide a variety of educational
materials and toys and did not think it was important for nursery
school teachers to teach social rules or skills. Teachers describing their programs as having no particular curriculum
heavily endorsed the need to provide love and affection and to
actively socialize children; they did not mention the need to
provide for educational materials and toys or the need for

discipline and management. Those teachers describing their
programs as eclectic showed, appropriately, diverse goals and
their votes yielded moderate levels of endorsement for all the
goals presented.

Day Care Centers

Day care centers were the last form of day care we observed. They are basically similar to nursery schools except
that they offer full-time care. Often their activities and schedule overlap with the nursery school's but are extended to more
than eight hours by meals, naps, and free play. Day care
centers are used by about 13 percent of working mothers of
preschool children in the U.S. today.

In our study, day care center programs were indistinguishable from nursery school programs in most respects. This was
particularly true for measures of the physical environment, but
indices of the social environment were also very similar. The
only significant difference was in the adult-child ratio reported
by the teacher or director: 1 to 6 in nursery schools and 1 to 4
in full-day centers. Since there was no difference in the adult-
child ratios observed in classrooms, however, it is likely that
this apparent difference resulted from the teachers' including
in their ratio calculation some ancillary personnel (e.g., cooks
or custodians) or a second shift of teachers and aides, required
by these whole-day programs.

The few features that did differentiate nursery schools
and day care centers were characteristics of the caregivers.
Day care center teachers were the youngest group in our study
(an average age of just 30 years) and had been working in the
centers in which they were observed an average of 2-1/2 years,
a shorter period of time than teachers in nursery schools.
Otherwise, teachers, children, curricula, and the physical
environment were not significantly different for nursery school
and day care center programs.

The major difference between nursery school and day care
center experiences, then, is in the number of hours the child
is in the day care setting rather than in the features of the
program to which he or she is exposed. In our study, the
typical day care center subject was at the center 8 hours every
day while the nursery schooler was at the center less than 3
hours a day.

Day Care Forms and Children's Competence

Clearly, there are substantial and documentable differences
among the four forms of day care—babysitters, day care homes,
nursery schools, and day care centers—differences in the physical setting, the social milieu, the characteristics of the caregiver,
and the activities children engage in. It would be reasonable
to expect that such differences would be related to the development of intellectual competence and social skills in the children
attending the day care programs. To examine this possibility
we used measures of children's performance in standard structured or semistructured assessments at home and in our laboratory
playroom.

For our "laboratory" assessments children came with their
mothers individually to a room at the University. Despite its
one way window, the room gave the appearance of a comfortable
livingroom, with an oriental rug, pictures, toys, comfortable
chairs for the mothers, and child-sized table and chairs for
the children. Each child and mother first went through an
hour-long series of assessments which included episodes of
free play with the toys provided, interactions with an unfamiliar
woman and man, tests of the child's knowledge of sex roles,
verbal labels, and perspective taking, several brief separations
from mother, and simulated affective incidents in which mother
or stranger acted distressed or helpless. At the completion of
these assessments another child of the same age, sex, and in
the same type of care arrangement arrived, and the two children
were given opportunities during the next hour to interact, play,
converse, and cooperate, with each other and a variety of toys.
Similar assessments were conducted in the child's home, and in
addition, in that setting, ratings were made of the child's social
behavior during an evening meal with the whole family. Observers, strangers, and examiners were, as far as possible,
blind to the child's care arrangement. The following measures
are based on these laboratory and home assessments.

●Proximity to mother: Child-initiated physical contact and
proximity to the mother in the lab session,
after brief separations or when adult
stranger was present.

●Sociability to
mother: Positive, reciprocal, social interaction
with mother during free play, coopera-
tion in joint tasks, positive interaction
and greeting after brief separations,

	and comforting after the mother "hurt" herself, in the laboratory session.
•Social cognition:	Ability to take the perspective—visual and conceptual—of another person, to communicate nonegocentrically, to apply appropriate labels to emotional stories, and to identify objects as preferred by girls or boys.
•Social competence with adult stranger:	Friendliness, cooperativeness, comforting, helping, and trust, with unfamiliar adults in the laboratory.
•Social competence with peer stranger:	Positive interaction—talking, playing, showing affection, and cooperating—in joint tasks and in free play with toys with unfamiliar age-mate in the laboratory.
•Negative behavior to peer stranger:	Negative behavior—taking away toys, controlling, insulting, refusing, with-drawing, or avoiding—the unfamiliar peer in the laboratory.
•Social competence at home:	Obedience, self confidence, sociability, autonomy, assertiveness, playfulness, cheerfulness, and nonaggression displayed during an unstructured observational session at home at dinnertime.
•Cognition:	Language comprehension, verbal fluency, object recognition, knowledge of concepts, and digit span, assessed in standard tests.

All but the last two of these measures were collected twice for each child, one year apart. Scores for the measure "Negative to Peer Stranger" were not systematically related to children's increasing age; all others were found to decrease (Proximity to Mother) or increase (all the rest) systematically with age, supporting our expectation that these standard assessments would reflect children's developing levels of competence. The parallel sets of measures were kept separate in the analyses of day care forms and features, in order to investigate the degree of consistency in the relations observed.

In order to investigate the question of whether these indices of competence were related to the form of day care in

which the child was placed, analyses of variance were carried
out on the measures. Results of these analyses are summarized
in Table 2.1.

These results show that children attending nursery-school
programs were the most developmentally advanced of the children
in the study. They scored consistently highest on assessments
of cognition, social cognition, and social competence with adults,
and relatively higher on sociability with mother and social competence with peer and lower on negative behavior to the peer
(significantly different from the babysitter group in the second
year assessment). Least advantaged were children with in-home
babysitters: They never scored highest on a test and they were
significantly more likely than day care center children to behave
negatively toward the peer, significantly less likely than day
care home children to interact positively with the peer, and
significantly lower than nursery-school children in competence
overall. Children in day care homes had the distinction of
scoring highest on social competence with a peer (in the first
year) and maintaining the closest physical proximity to mother.
Children from day care centers maintained significantly greater
physical distance from their mothers, but this physical distance
was accompanied by significantly higher verbal sociability toward
mother, both in the laboratory assessment and at home at dinnertime.

Thus we see that the four forms of day care we observed
had distinct patterns of competence that could be logically associated with their respective "ecologies." The explicitly educational orientation of the nursery school was reflected in children's
advanced cognition and adult-oriented competence. The lengthier
daily separation of mothers and children using full-time day
care centers was reflected in their greater physical independence
from mother coupled with more involved social interactions with
her. Children from day care homes, who had less familiarity
than day care center children with an "institutional" setting,
stayed closer than center children to their mothers in our
assessment room at the university, but, coincident with their
greater daily opportunities for social interaction with agemates,
played more comfortably, cooperatively, and actively with an
unfamiliar peer than children with in-home babysitters. Children
with untrained babysitters in their own homes, with, at most,
one other child, who was usually younger, and with no educational program, did not excel in any domain of competence.

These patterns of development in different day care forms
give us some clues about what we might expect as the result of
a child's being in either sitter or center day care. But as we

Table 2.1 Analyses of Variance for Child Competence Measures in Different Forms of Day Care[1]

Child Competence Measures	Means				Contrasts[2]					
	In-home Sitter	Day-care Home	Nursery School	Day-care Center	In-home vs. Day-care Home	In-home vs. Nursery School	In-home vs. Day-care Center	Day-care Home vs. Nursery School	Day-care Home vs. Day-care Center	Nursery School vs. Day-care Center
Year 1	(n=14)	(n=20)	(n=22)	(n=25)						
Social Cognition	.13	-.08	.62	.15		.10				
Proximity to Mother	.08	.80	-.45	-1.01				.08	.01	
Sociability to Mother	-.12	-1.13	-.22	.83					.10	
Social Competence with Peer	.62	1.23	.69	.47	.04			.03	.06	
Negative to Peer	.36	-.31	.01	.41						
Social Competence with Adult	.22	.08	1.24	.20						
Cognition	.69	.67	1.00	.64						
Social Competence at Home	.05	-.25	.32	-.04				.03		.03
Social Competence with Visitor	.10	-.91	1.29	.27				.09		
Year 2	(n=6)	(n=7)	(n=39)	(n=31)						
Social Cognition	-.49	-.26	.35	-.62		.09				
Proximity to Mother	-.40	-.09	.33	-.71		.10				
Sociability to Mother	-1.83	-.21	.68	-.46				.04		.04
Social Competence with Peer	-.34	-1.19	-.23	.29		.07				
Negative Behavior to Peer	1.77	-.49	-.40	.29		.05	.01			
Social Competence with Adult	-1.41	-1.99	1.31	-.07		.08				
Social Competence at Home	.670	.688	.682	.692				.03	.10	.05

[1] Child's age co-varied out.
[2] p levels, all p values ≤ .10 shown.

have suggested, each of these day care "forms" contains a myriad of "features," which vary from sitter to sitter and center to center. In the next section we explore how features of particular day care settings are related to the development of children in them.

CHILDREN'S COMPETENCE AND FEATURES OF THE DAY CARE SETTING

Day care settings vary in size and shape and quality, not only across different day care forms but within a single form. In the preceding sections we stressed commonalities across settings by discussing means and mean differences for the four day care forms. In this section we explore the significance of different day care features by examining correlations between children's scores on assessments of social and intellectual competence and characteristics of their particular day care settings. This was done separately for home settings (combining in-home babysitter and day care home groups) and center settings (combining nursery-school and day care center groups). Results of these analyses are presented in Tables 2.2 and 2.3 respectively.

Home Settings

The features of day care settings that we assessed can be divided roughly into three categories: the composition of the group of people present in the setting, the personal qualities of the caregiver, and attributes of the physical setting.

Group Composition

In this category one feature we expected to be related to children's social competence with peers was the number of children present in the day care setting, since these two variables were both higher for children in day care homes than with in-home sitters. Surprisingly, however, the correlation between them at the level of individual settings and scores was non-significant. The reason some children are precocious in social skills with peers is not, it seems, simply because they have more children around them during the day. Instead, there may be some optimal number of children that fosters the development of social skills. Having either no other children to play with or "too many" (more than five) was associated with low

Table 2.2 Correlations between Features of Home Day-Care Settings and Children's Competence[1]

Day-Care Features	Child Competence Measures								
	Social Cognition	Cognition	Proximity to Mother	Sociability to Mother	Social Competence with Peer	Negative Behavior to Peer	Social Competence with Adult	Social Competence with Visitor	Social Competence at Home
Group Composition									
Adults		-.39		.43					
Children									
Men					.36				-.45
Younger Children				-.33					
Ratio (Ch/Cg)									
Heterogeneity									
SES									
Caregiver Qualities									
Education								.41	
Training									
Age		.37						-.35	
Agree with Experts					.46				
Physical Environment									
Toys									
Structure	.59	.53					.63		
Decorations		-.46					-.51		
Danger						.38	.59		-.36
Mess		-.47							-.48

[1]Partial correlations with child's age partialled out, for year 1 assessments (n=29); sample was too small to use in correlational year 2 analyses. Table shows all coefficients significant at $p \le .05$.

Table 2.3 Correlations between Features of Center Day-Care Programs and Children's Competence[1]

Child Competence Measures

Day Care Features	Cognition	Social Cognition		Proximity to Mother		Sociability to Mother		Social Competence with Peer		Negative Behavior to Peer		Social Competence with Adult		Social Competence with Visitor	Social Competence at Home	
		Yr1	Yr2	Yr1	Yr2	Yr1	Yr2	Yr1	Yr2	Yr1	Yr2	Yr1	Yr2		Yr1	Yr2
Group Composition																
Adults		.28					-.24						-.43			
Men			-.37	-.44	.58		-.32			.33				-.28		-.44
Children in center		.36									-.36			-.33		
Children in class				-.29				-.28			-.32					
Older Children	.41	.31	.28								-.42					-.35
Younger Children			-.29		.37		.24				-.53	-.29		-.22		
Ratio (Ch/T)					.28				.29		-.22		.32			
Heterogeneity		-.28			.31				-.30		-.26			-.40		
SES	.26	-.25	-.31				-.31		-.28	-.25	-.29	-.48				
Teacher Characteristics																
Education	.24	.24			.30				.49					-.32	.41	-.28
Training	.22			.31				-.31	-.28							
Age			.35									.24		.23	-.34	.27
Agree with Experts		.25		.34			.24		-.49				-.27			
Time in Setting			.23											.33		-.31
Physical Environment																
Toys	.27	.34			-.34		-.25	-.28	-.26					.33	-.30	
Structure	.29		.28											.29		
Decorations	.27			.28		.29							-.37	-.33		-.30
Danger			-.25					-.31						-.26		
Mess		-.32	-.49						.26		-.33		-.30	-.32	-.30	

[1]Partial correlations with child's age partialled out (n=47 to 70). Table shows all r's significant at $p \leq .05$.

social competence with the peer. The social composition variable that was linearly correlated with social competence with a peer was the amount of time a man was present in the setting. Since men are known to interact with children more as active and stimulating playmates than as physical caretakers (e.g., Clarke-Stewart, 1978) this feature might well have encouraged playful interaction among the children and thus fostered their social competence. Having a man present may be a mixed blessing, however; children in day care settings with a man present were inclined to be less compliant, confident, and cheerful when we observed them at dinnertime.

Correlations with other compositional features were either not statistically significant or not consistently positive or negative. The number of children present, their heterogeneity in terms of age, sex, ethnicity, and family socioeconomic level, and the ratio of children to adults (features which have been shown to be associated with children's behavior in day care centers, see Clarke-Stewart and Fein, 1983) were not significantly related to any measures of child competence. The number of older children present (also a significant predictor in center settings) could not be examined here because none of our home day care settings included older children. The number of younger children, however, was significantly related to the child's sociability with mother: the presence of more young children in the day care setting predicted lower sociability with mother in the laboratory. No explanation for this correlation, or for the only other significant associations (between the number of adults in the setting and high sociability to mother and low social cognition) seems obvious. Perhaps we just have to attribute these significant correlations to chance.

Caregiver Qualities

The next set of features to be examined are the personal qualities and characteristics of the caregiver. Here we find several interpretable correlations with children's competence. One reasonable correlation was that between a higher level of social competence for the child (with a visitor to the home) and a higher level of education for the caregiver. Another is between a higher level of social competence with a peer for the child and a higher level of agreement with child development "experts" for the caregiver. This measure of caregivers' knowledge about child development and child rearing (which did not differentiate between caregivers in different forms of day care) was based on suggested solutions to hypothetical problems that might arise in rearing a child. It reflected an

attitude that included encouraging play among children: e.g.,
"What should a mother do if her 3-year old always wanted to
play with an older sister's toys whenever the sister was playing
with them?" (Praise them for playing together with a toy.
Teach them to take turns.) "What should a parent do if a
7-year old doesn't seem to have any friends?" (Join an after-
school playgroup or club with the child. Take her to the park.
Invite other children over to the house.) It may be that caregivers scoring higher on this measure were more likely to
actively encourage children's play, and that this was a significant feature of the day care environment for fostering social
skills.

These two significant correlations support the more general
notion that children do better in day care settings with more
qualified caregivers. Unfortunately, however, we found no
significant correlations between children's competence and caregivers' training in child development—a feature one might
expect would be a better index of the kind of "professionalism"
found in other research (Fosburg, 1981; Espinosa, 1980) to
be related to more active involvement by home caregivers.
Perhaps this was because in our study so few caregivers had
had much training (only two had had as many as six courses
in child development). Even more unfortunately, the magnitude
of the two significant correlations we did find (with caregiver
education and agreement with experts) was reduced to non-
significance when the variance attributable to the child's family
socioeconomic background was statistically controlled. In a
descriptive field study like this one, one cannot separate the
contributions of day care features from those of family factors
which contribute directly or indirectly to children's development.
We can only note here that in our "real world" sample of day
care users and settings those home day care children who ac-
quired social and intellectual skills earlier had caregivers who
were more highly educated and more likely to agree with current
expert opinion on child rearing.

The final caregiver feature to be examined was age. Children under the supervision of older caregivers (over 50) were
highly successful in the tests of social perspective taking, but
children with younger caregivers were more socially competent
in their actual interactions with adult strangers who came to
visit them. A possible explanation for this is that grandmotherly
caregivers provided more sedentary care which was intellectually
informative but not socially stimulating whereas younger caregivers were both more like the graduate student strangers who
came to visit and more active in their play with the children in

ways that might have fostered their interactional skills. We are currently analyzing extensive observational records of the children's behavior in their various settings and we expect that these analyses of the actual patterns of interaction in different day care settings will illuminate these relations.

Physical Environment

The final set of features in these day care settings pertains to the physical environment. A pattern of significant correlations here suggests that children are most likely to benefit from a home day care setting where the physical environment is organized around and for them. When the setting and the schedule are structured so that there are areas and times set aside for play, when the environment is kept relatively neat and orderly, when there are fewer adult-oriented decorative items (and so less need for restrictions "Stay away from those records." "Don't touch that plant." "Oh, look, you've knocked over your mommy's vase!"), children quite consistently score higher on measures of social and intellectual competence. On the other hand, just providing more toys and materials per se, within the limits observed in our home day care settings, does not make a difference in children's development. Children in homes where we observed more physical danger were more "fearless"—they were more aggressive toward an unfamiliar peer, less compliant with their parents, and more outgoing with an unfamiliar adult.

Lest the reader leap to the conclusion that the physical environment directly causes these differences in children's competence, it should be noted that, as with the correlations with caregiver qualities, the magnitude of correlations of physical features with cognitive measures was reduced to non-significance when family socioeconomic status was statistically controlled—suggesting that these correlational associations may be at least in part due to the parents' selection of particular, more or less structured, settings for their children.

Center Programs

Whereas features of home day care settings were of quite limited help in predicting children's competence, as the abundance of statistically significant correlation coefficients in Table 2.3 shows, features of center settings were substantially more useful.

Group Composition

First, there was significant predictability from the number and kind of people present at the center. Paralleling the results in sitter-care arrangements, we found evidence contradicting the simple adage that "bigger is better." Correlations in center-care arrangements showed that larger centers had children who generally did more poorly (specifically, lower in social cognition, sociability to mother, and social competence at home). More people in the child's particular class, either adults or children, similarly, was associated with lower levels of social competence (with adults and peers).

But one cannot propose replacing "bigger is better" with "bigger is badder," either, because although these negative relations were found, there were also some positive ones: children in larger classes in the first year of the study (at ages 2 and 3) did better on tests of social perspective or role taking. Perhaps having more different adults and children around gave these young children more opportunity to observe and learn, first, that other people have their own viewpoints that may differ from the child's—it is impossible to remain egocentrically naive in a large group—and, second, that these people have consistent and predictable emotional responses and play preferences—e.g., all adults are happy when they are kissed; all boys like playing with trucks.

This knowledge apparently was not translated into a higher level of cooperative action with others, however—quite the reverse. Being with a crowd of children in the day care center may have encouraged the child to look out for "number one" in an interaction with an unfamiliar peer; a choice of teachers at school may have allowed the child to get by with a less cooperative attitude toward adults. Social knowledge was not additionally advanced if the class was very heterogeneous, either. Being in a more diverse class (in terms of ethnicity, age, and socioeconomic status) was associated with having a lower level of social knowledge. Perhaps too much diversity hindered the generalizations that were necessary in our tests of social cognition.

A high degree of heterogeneity in the composition of the class was related to lower levels of competence on other measures as well: less independence from mother, less social competence with a peer and with an adult visitor. But heterogeneity and class size (also center size), number of younger children and number of children per teacher—all the indices of the presence of a larger group of children) did have one advantage: children from these programs were less likely to behave negatively toward

the unfamiliar peer in the second year laboratory assessment.
One possible explanation of this consistent relation is that with
a larger group of children, aggressive behavior—chaos—in the
day care setting cannot be tolerated. Teachers may more actively
discourage children from negative behavior with their playmates
when there are more of them around. Some support for this
explanation comes from the finding that when there were more
children per caregiver, children were also observed in the
laboratory to be more cooperative with adults and children.
This may not fit with the notion of the benefits presumed to
accrue from a high adult-child ratio, but it fits with the image
of the lone teacher exerting tight control over her large class—
"Take turns. No pushing. No hitting. Do what I tell you.
Be good children. Play together with the wagon." In contrast
to the picture of this tight control the presence of men in the
setting was related to higher levels of aggressive behavior with
peers.

The presence of older children in the class was related to
advanced development of children's independence and intellect,
and the predominance of younger children in the class to re-
tarded development of independence, social cognition, and social
competence with an adult. Older children may serve as models
of mature thought and behavior; younger children may model
less mature behavior and consume the teacher's attention.

Finally, there were associations with the socioeconomic
level of families whose children were in the class. With a higher
proportion of middle- and upper-middle class children in the
class, children were more cognitively advanced, more competent
with adults, and less negative with peers; when more classmates were from more lower- and working-class families children
were more sociable with their mothers and more socially competent
with peers. These two sets of correlations may reflect middle-
and lower-class values. They do not suggest that putting a
poor child into a middle-class nursery school will make him into
a middle-class child, however; when the individual child's
socioeconomic status was statistically controlled, in these
analyses, correlations between the socioeconomic status of the
class and measures of children's cognition, negative behavior
to the peer, and social competence with an adult were no longer
significant.

Teacher Characteristics

Predictability from variables reflecting the characteristics
of the teacher, which are commonly held to be the most critical
aspects of the day care experience, was disappointing. True,

there were some predictable associations: children who had
caregivers who were older, more stable (had been in the center
longer), more highly trained in child development, and agreed
with the experts' opinion about child rearing did better in our
cognitive tests, for example (although the relations with training and agreement with experts were not significant when family
background was taken into account). But children with better
trained caregivers were also less independent and socially competent with peers, parents, and other adults. Perhaps this was
because teachers with more academic training in child development focussed on children's academic education to the detriment
of their social skills. It was children with caregivers who had
a higher general level of education rather than specific training
in early childhood education who, although they were not advanced in cognition or competence with an adult visitor, were
more competent with peers and more close, compliant, and
cheerful with parents both in our playroom and at home.

Physical Environment

Relations between child development measures and features
of the physical environment were quite sensible: children who
did well on our tests of intellectual abilities were in day care
environments that were safe, orderly, and cognitively stimulating—
rich in toys, educational materials, and decorations of all kinds,
appropriately organized into separate activity areas. Children
who were especially competent with an adult stranger were in
environments that were also safe and orderly, but "play oriented"
rather than visually stimulating—rich in toys but low in adult
decorations. Children whose social skills with peers were
advanced tended to be in day care environments that were safe,
too, but were messy and had relatively few toys. Although we
cannot establish causal direction in this self selected sample,
these correlations did not become nonsignificant when family
socioeconomic status was partialled out, and it does seem reasonable to suggest that a safe physical environment is a basic
minimum requirement for a good day care program, that rich
materials and an organized play area foster intellectual development, and that when cognitively stimulating toys are not readily
available children become more engaged with peers, playing
freely and messily, and thus sharpening their social skills.

Curriculum

The final feature of the day care program to be analyzed
was the educational component. As well as calculating correla-

tions of child competence scores with the degree of program
"structure" we performed analyses of variance for curriculum
groups on each of our child development measures. Consistent
with previous research, results in this study suggest that
although children's cognitive scores were positively related to
the degree of structure in the program—to having organized
activities and routines and so on—there was no relation between
this index of child development and the particular curriculum
the program followed: "traditional," "eclectic," Montessori,
Piagetian, or "none." Nor was there a significant relation with
social competence with peers. The only association with the
curriculum was that children from "traditional" programs and
those following no formal curriculum were most socially competent with the unfamiliar adult, whereas those in Montessori and
Piagetian programs were least competent. The explanation for
this may lie in the teachers' respective goals: traditional and
non-curriculum teachers stressed the importance of socializing
and actively teaching children social skills; Piagetian and
Montessori teachers never mentioned these as goals of their
programs.

Conclusion

In a sense, our findings validate the concerns of the
hypothetical parent in our introduction, who must select a day
care arrangement from a myriad of confusing possibilities.
From our earliest efforts to design this study to our latest
analyses of its data we have been reminded of the enormous
complexity of the day care scene. Day care does indeed come
in diverse and odd-shaped packages of fluctuating features,
and there is no uniform "day care experience" for a child or
his family.

At the most general level, the child's day care experience
is determined by the structure or form of the day care arrangement. By examining differences among the four forms of day
care we had selected for this study—in-home sitters, day care
homes, nursery schools, and day care centers—we were able
to describe several distinct patterns of early childhood experience and associated patterns of child and adult behavior. Day
care provided by a babysitter in the child's own home we found
to be informal, homey, and grandmotherly, exposing the child
to neither other children nor an educational program. Children
receiving this kind of care were the least developmentally advanced of the children we observed. Day care provided in a

sitter's home was also informal and homey, but the caregivers
tended to be younger, better educated, and about half the time
had a modest amount of training in child development. Children
in day care homes were exposed to an average of four other
young children. Children in this form of day care were developmentally advanced in one area only: they were more socially
skilled and cooperative with unfamiliar peers at ages 2 and 3.
Day care in a nursery school or day care center differed
dramatically from that in home care arrangements. There were
more children around and more caregivers; activities were more
structured and systematically educational; caregivers were
more highly educated and trained in child development. The
children in nursery-school programs were most developmentally
advanced in all areas. The physical setting and social milieu
in full-time day care centers and part-time nursery schools
were not different, but teachers in the former tended to be
younger and had been working at the centers a shorter time.
Day care center children were not as advanced as nursery
school children cognitively—suggesting that simply "more" of
a center program is not necessarily advantageous—but compared
to home care children, they showed a more advanced relationship with their mothers (more physically independent but more
verbally sociable). Thus the study suggested that there are
links between the ecology of day care forms and children's
developmental patterns.

Moving from the level of group differences to individual
differences, we also found links between specific features of
day care settings and the developmental level of children in
these settings. Children who were more competent with unfamiliar peers were likely to be in home day care settings with
a small number of other children, a man, and a sitter who was
(relative to other sitters) knowledgeable about child development and child rearing, or in center-care settings with a small
homogeneous class of lower-class children, a physical environment that was safe but messy and disorganized rather than
educationally stimulating, and a teacher, who (relative to other
teachers) did not have very much training and knowledge about
child development. Children who were more socially competent
with unfamiliar adults were likely to be in home day-care settings
with a caregiver who had been to college and was in her 30's
or 40's, or in center programs in a small class with a caregiver
who was in her 30's or 40's and who stressed social rather than
cognitive skills. Children who were advanced cognitively were
likely to be in home day care settings that were structured and
organized, or center settings in which activities were structured

and organized, and, in addition, there was a wealth of toys and decorations, the caregiver was trained and knowledgeable about child development, and there were older children and more people in the class.

It is tempting to interpret links between environment and development—at the level of form and group or feature and individual—as suggesting that the environment has caused the differences in development: that a structured program or a trained caregiver has facilitated cognitive development, for example. Tempting—but wrong. We cannot establish causal direction from a descriptive study such as this one. We can state only that within the real-world limits of self selection the observed associations exist. The real test of causal direction must be made experimentally, by systematically manipulating the environmental features that this descriptive study suggests may be linked to developmental outcomes. Caregiver training in child development is one feature the Chicago Study suggests would be worthy of investigation. On the basis of correlational data, investigators in the National Day Care Study (Ruopp et al., 1979) suggested that caregiver training is one of two major day care variables that affect children's development, and in the present study, too, caregiver training was a significant predictor of the cognitive level of children attending center-based programs. However, a number of qualifications of this finding underline the need to explore the potential positive influence of caregiver training experimentally. First the power of caregiver training to predict a child's cognitive competence was substantially diminished when the child's family's socioeconomic status was statistically controlled. Second, caregiver training predicted cognitive scores only for 2- and 3-year olds, and not for 3- and 4-year olds. And, third, caregiver training was significantly correlated with children's cognitive and social development only in center care arrangements and not in home day care arrangements. When experiments varying caregiver training are performed, moreover, it would behoove the researcher to manipulate not only the amount or length of such training but also its content. For our study also suggested that an academic focus associated with a high level of training in child development might affect children's social competence with peers detrimentally.

Beyond providing specific suggestions of variables worthy of experimental investigation, the present study also offers more general suggestions about the design and interpretation of experimental research in this area. The study makes patently clear that day care in the real world is varied, complex, and multidimensional. In designing experimental treatments and comparisons, therefore, experimenters will need to be vigilant to a multitude of factors. Qualities of the physical environment, characteristics of the caregiver, and the composition of participants will all need to be considered and controlled. Nor will the experimenter necessarily reap rewards from the conventional manipulation of variables one at a time. The whole day care experience may indeed be greater than the sum of its parts, and to show effects it may be necessary for investigators to compare experimental treatments that include features combined into the "packages" identified as relevant by naturalistic studies like this one. There may well be effects that show up only when substantially different packages like different day care forms are contrasted. Experimenters will also need to be cautious about generalizing the results of their treatments to unexamined settings. Clear differences in the predictability of particular features were found in the present study, for example, depending on whether they were assessed in home or center settings. Naturalistic field studies like the Chicago Study of Child Care and Development inform us about the state of real day care experiences today and point the way to more sophisticated experimentation and explanation tomorrow.

REFERENCES

Clarke-Stewart, K. A. And daddy makes three: The father's impact on mother and young child. Child Development, 1978, 49, 466-478.

Clarke-Stewart, K. A., and Fein, G. G. Early childhood programs. In P. H. Mussen (Ed.), Handbook of child psychology (fourth edition). Volume 2. J. Campos and M. Haith (Eds.), Infancy and developmental psychobiology. New York, NY: John Wiley & Sons, 1983.

Espinosa, L. An ecological study of family day care. Unpublished doctoral dissertation, University of Chicago, 1980.

Fosburg, S. Family day care in the United States: Summary of findings. Washington, D.C.: U.S. Dept. of Health and Human Services (Publication No. OHDS 80-30282), 1981.

Ruopp, R., Travers, J., Glantz, F., and Coelen, C. Children at the center. Cambridge, MA: ABT Associates, 1979.

3.

Day Care and Early Socialization: The Role of Maternal Attitude

Mark D. Everson, Lela Sarnat, and Sueann R. Ambron

Historically, the family has provided the earliest human environment within which the child's character is shaped (Kardiner, 1947). It is here that early patterns of compliance with authority are established. It is here that the child learns to curb his impulses and to adopt culturally appropriate ways of behaving. It is in the context of the family that the child makes the journey from an immature, self-centered organism to a mature, socialized adult.

Recent history has witnessed a decline of the family as the primary agent of socialization in Western society. Today, because of various economic and social factors, including a broadening of the traditional role of women in society, institutional and group settings share many of the socializing and enculturative responsibilities that were once the near-exclusive province of the family. The influence of such settings is rapidly extending downward as mothers of younger children are returning to work and relying on non-familial day care providers to take greater responsibility for the upbringing of their children.

Critics have objected to the use of day care for young children, cautioning that extended periods of time in group

This research was supported by the National Science Foundation under Grant BNS 78-09195-A2, the National Institute of Health under Grants 1R01-MH-31586-02 and 5R01-MH-31586-03, and by the Stanford Center for the Study of Youth Development.

settings may produce the "day care personality"—that is, a
pattern of behavior characterized by uncooperative, noncompli-
ant interactions with adults, increased aggression toward peers,
reduced impulse control, and a limited attention span. Several
processes have been suggested by which day care may alter
the usual course of socialization. First, day care providers
are likely to differ from parents as socializing agents (Kagan,
Kearsley, and Zelazo, 1978). Many providers, particularly
those with formal training in child development, are likely to
hold a more permissive approach to childrearing than do most
parents. They are also less likely to be psychologically invested
in their child charges or to view behavioral immaturity as a
personal reflection on them. As a result, compared to parents,
hired caregivers are usually more tolerant of noncompliance,
aggression, behavioral immaturity, and other deviations from
strict adult standards. In settings with inadequate adult-child
ratios, caregivers have excessive demands on their time, often
preventing them from intervening to shape the child's behavior
even when they deem it appropriate to do so. Furthermore,
when adult caregivers abdicate responsibility for teaching appropriate behavior, either intentionally or by default, it is likely
that the child's peer group will assume that role.

Group settings may also inadvertently encourage aggression
and other negative behaviors because adults are more likely to
respond to and thus reinforce such behaviors in situations in
which children must compete for adult attention. Yet another
factor is that most day care centers (and portions of many
family day care homes) are designed primarily as child care
facilities. In an essentially child-proofed environment, fewer
restrictions and limitations are required to protect property
and to maintain the safety of the young child. Day care children
may therefore have fewer opportunities to master their impulses
and to learn behavior appropriate to a wider range of settings.

Another avenue by which day care may hinder appropriate
socialization is by undermining the socializing role of parents.
It is believed that effective socialization depends upon a strong
affective bond between the infant and his/her mother or primary
attachment figure (Ainsworth et al., 1978). Such a relationship
increases both the salience of the mother as a model and the
reinforcement potency of her efforts to shape his/her behavior
(Lamb, 1978). In other words, if the child is dependent upon
and emotionally involved with her, the mother is better able to
persuade him/her to adopt parental standards. Dilution of the
attachment relationship because of extended periods of time in
day care raises the specter of an aggressive, disobedient child

who will "spurn the values his parents cherish" (Kagan et al., 1978).

These concerns about the effects of day care on early socialization have prompted a great deal of research. (See the excellent review by Jay Belsky in this volume). Although these results are far from conclusive, there is substantial evidence that children with early day care experience, especially in group settings, may be less well socialized to adult norms than children without such experience. Research has shown, for example, that children with extended day care experience beginning at an early age are physically and verbally more aggressive toward adults and peers (Schwarz, Strickland, and Krolick, 1974), less cooperative with adults (Schwarz et al., 1974), less coopera- tive with peers (Lippman and Grote, 1974), and less compliant to their mothers (Rubenstein, Howes, and Boyle, 1981). They have also been rated as less tolerant of frustration (Schwarz et al., 1974) and have been observed to display more frequent temper tantrums (Rubenstein et al., 1981). In individual testing sessions, children with early day care center experience have been found to be less enthusiastic, less attentive, and less socially responsive to the examiner (Schwarz, 1983). Kinder- garten and elementary school-age children with day care histories are more likely to be identified as troublemakers by their class- mates (Barton and Schwarz, 1981) and by their teachers (Robert- son, 1982).

On the other hand, several other investigators have either failed to find more frequent negative or inappropriate behavior among day care children (e.g., Golden et al., 1978; Macrae and Herbert-Johnson, 1975) or have found more mature levels of social functioning among such children. For example, Clarke- Stewart (1983) compared 2- to 4-year olds in a range of day care settings with those who were cared for at home. Children in day care, particularly those in center care, were observed to be more cooperative and compliant and to have more frequent positive interactions both with their own mothers and with strangers. Gunnarson (1978) studied 5-year olds in Sweden who had been cared for in centers, family day care homes, or exclusively by their parents at home since infancy. Children reared in day care centers were found to be more compliant and cooperative with peers and no less negative in their inter- actions with adults than children cared for in their own or in day care homes.

We can only speculate why research in this area has been so contradictory. One plausible explanation, as Belsky and Steinberg (1978) have suggested, is that the socialization effects

of day care may not be inherent in day care per se, but may
depend upon the specific educational and child management
practices employed in the day care setting and that these practices depend in part on community and societal values. A
second explanation centers around design limitations in many
studies. With few exceptions, prior studies have relied on
posttest only or retrospective designs which assume initial
comparability between day care and parent care groups. Yet,
this may not be a valid assumption. The values and attitudes
of families using day care are likely to differ in several respects
from those of families not using day care (e.g., Hock, 1978).
Furthermore, Roopnarine and Lamb (1978, 1980) have found
that, at least among preschool-age samples, there may be stable
differences in mother-child interaction among children about to
enter day care and those who are remaining at home.

The work of Cronbach and Snow (1977) on aptitude-
treatment interactions provides another explanation for the
inconsistency of research in this area. They argue that conflict-
ing findings (especially among studies of low statistical power)
suggest the possibility of higher-order interactions which
remain undetected. In other words, the significant main effects
of treatment (i.e. day care) reported in some studies may
actually be undetected interactions between subject and treatment variables. This argument can easily be applied to the day
care literature. Prior research has focused almost exclusively
on the global effect of "Day Care" on "The Child". Little
attention has been given to the question of whether the effect
of day care is uniform for young children, or whether the
specific impact depends upon individual characteristics of the
child or family.

The Stanford Day Care Study was undertaken with these
issues in mind. It was designed to examine the effects of center
and family day care on the early social development and attachment behavior of 1- and 2-year old children. In particular,
we were interested in the possible role of the maternal attitude
toward day care in mediating the impact of day care. During
initial pilot work for the study, we were impressed by the
wide variation in maternal feelings about using day care.
Some mothers were extremely reluctant to entrust the care of
their children to others, believing that doing so would be detrimental to their development and emotional security. Many held
the view that a mother's place is at home with her children.
Leaving the care of their children to others would indicate
that they were inadequate or "bad" mothers. When, because

of economic or family circumstances, these mothers were forced to use day care, they often suffered intense anxiety and guilt.

Other mothers seemed to have absolutely no concerns or doubts about the value of day care. They believed that day care would be a positive, growth-enhancing experience for their children. In their minds, the opportunity for their children to interact with peers and to benefit from structured educational activities far outweighed any disadvantages. These mothers often felt that the care their children would receive in day care would be as good, if not better, than the care they themselves could provide. Many such mothers viewed day care as a normal, everyday aspect of a child's life—much like going to the grocery store.

We speculated that the attitudes expressed by these mothers might be essential to our understanding of the specific impact of day care and the young child's overall course of development for three reasons. First, the maternal attitude toward day care may be a gross indicator of the closeness or intensity of the mother-child relationship. Mothers who are apprehensive about placing their toddlers in day care may have closer or more intense relationships with them than mothers who do not share the same concerns about using day care. Second, mothers who feel anxious or guilty about using day care may be especially motivated to maintain their relationship with their children by compensating in some way for the lost time together. Third, maternal attitude toward day care may reflect maternal role satisfaction. Women who reluctantly use day care or who hold positive attitudes toward day care but stay at home may be in conflict over their role as caregiver/homemaker versus worker outside the home. Such role dissatisfaction may contribute to a loss of morale and self-esteem which may preclude sensitive mothering (Hoffman, 1974; Lamb, Owen, and Chase-Lansdale, 1979).

In addition to maternal attitude toward day care, we were also interested in investigating the role of four characteristics of the child in mediating the effect of day care: age at day care entry, gender, the amount of prior, non-parental care, and the stability of such arrangements. Anderson (1980) and Rutter (1979) among others, have speculated about the role of prior separation experience in influencing the impact of day care on individual children, although little research has been focused on this issue.

Another noteworthy aspect of our study was the use of pretesting prior to day care entry to ascertain the initial comparability of the day care and parent care groups. Pretesting consisted of a home visit and two laboratory sessions held on different days to reduce memory and fatigue effects. While pretesting before day care entry was an important feature of our design, it also proved to be a logistical nightmare. It was not unusual for us to learn on a Friday afternoon of a child who was to begin day care the following Monday morning. In spite of such time constraints, we "lost" relatively few children due to scheduling problems.

In addition to the pretesting, the study included an evaluation after 5 months and again after 10 months of day care. The first posttest consisted of a repeat of the two laboratory sessions held at pretesting. Posttest II consisted of a single laboratory session based in part on the earlier sessions. The study also included observations of the children in day care as a measure of the quality of care they received.

Although the study focused both on social development and attachment behavior, only the socialization results will be reported here. The findings on attachment as well as the analysis of the day care quality data are reported elsewhere (e.g., Everson et al., 1983). We were interested in a fairly diverse range of early socialization indices: response to adult authority, impulse control, prosocial behavior, and task-orientation. As a result, we included measures of compliance to the mother both with and without surveillance, compliance to and cooperation with unfamiliar adults, social responsiveness, response to frustration, willingness to share or help, persistence, task enthusiasm, and problem solving effectiveness.

SAMPLE DESCRIPTION

The sample consisted of 224 children between 12 and 24 months of age at the time they entered the study. The children were divided into three groups based upon the type of care they received between Pretesting and Posttest I five months later. Fifty-five of the children were enrolled in day care centers in the San Francisco Peninsula area for 20 to 50 hours per week (x = 34.2 hours). Sixty-two children entered family day care homes located in the same geographic area as the day care centers. They remained in family day care for 20 to 50 hours per week (x = 34.6 hours). These two groups formed the Center Day Care (CDC) and Family Day Care (FDC) groups, respectively. Six CDC children changed centers between Pretesting and Posttest I, while 20 FDC children switched FDC

arrangements at least once during this period. Another 100
children did not attend day care but were cared for by their
mothers at home. These children constitute the Parent Care
group (PC). Finally, the sample included 7 children who
changed from CDC to FDC or from FDC to CDC during their
first 5 months of care. They were not included in any comparisons of the three major childrearing samples.

Prior to pretesting, none of the children had attended
day care centers or had received more than minimal care after
the age of 6 months from unfamiliar persons. Some of the
children, however, had received a substantial amount of care
from relatives, friends of the family, or familiar babysitters
during the period from birth to pretesting. During the pretest
home visit, we interviewed mothers to obtain detailed information
about the amount of time the child had spent in the care of
others, as well as the number and familiarity of the caregivers
providing the care. A principal components factor analysis
was used to reduce the care history data into a smaller set of
variables. The analysis revealed two dominant factors accounting for 64 percent and 13 percent of the variance. Variables
assessing the total amount of time in supplemental care loaded
heavily on Factor 1. In Factor 2, the predominant variable was
the number of different individuals providing care. These
factors were labeled "Amount of Prior, Non-Parental Care"
and "Stability of Prior, Non-Parental Care", respectively.

We also interviewed mothers to ascertain their attitudes
toward day care. In the case of children who were about to
start day care, mothers were rated as positively disposed toward
day care or "Willing" if they expressed comfort or satisfaction
with their decisions to use day care. Mothers who expressed
regret or guilt about their decisions were rated as negatively
disposed toward day care or "Reluctant". Among the parent
care children, mothers were asked whether, and under what
circumstances, they would consider placing their children in
day care. Those voicing little or no reluctance to using day
care were rated as "Willing", while those who expressed opposi-
tion or strong reluctance were rated as "Reluctant".

Table 3.1 presents a comparison of the three childrearing
groups on maternal attitudes toward day care, amount and
stability of prior care, and a number of other demographic
variables. The groups were not significantly different from
one another on 11 of the 12 matching variables. The one
exception was amount of prior, non-parental care ($F[2,216] =$
12.60, $p < .001$). On the average, children in center day care
had received more supplemental care before pretesting than

Table 3.1 Demographics of Sample at Posttest I

	Center Day Care (N=55)	Family Day Care (N=62)	Parent Care (N=100)
Pretest Age	18.00	17.10	17.60
in Months[a]	(3.48)	(3.43)	(3.66)
Sex			
Percent Male	54	53	50
Percent Female	46	47	50
Ethnicity			
Percent Black	13	13	11
Percent White	76	74	77
Percent Hispanic	9	8	11
Percent Other	2	5	1
Amount of Prior,	.46	.05	-.32
Non-Parental Care[b]	(1.21)	(.95)	(.74)
Stability of Prior,	-.003	.02	.01
Non-Parental Care	.920	1.04	(1.00)
Birth Order			
Percent First Born	65	56	61
Percent Later Born	35	44	39
Number of Siblings Present in Home			
Percent with no Sibs	64	56	57
Percent with 1 to 2 Sibs	29	39	38
Percent with > 3 Sibs	7	5	5
Family Social	40.40	38.30	38.80
Status Index[c]	(11.62)	(13.95)	(15.81)
Family Composition			
Percent Intact	64	68	76
Percent Non-Intact	36	32	24
Maternal Age	25.40	25.50	25.30
at Parturition	(5.43)	(4.19)	(4.78)
Maternal Years	13.20	13.80	13.40
of Schooling	(2.21)	(1.90)	(1.96)
Maternal Attitude toward Day Care			
Percent Willing	56	45	60
Percent Reluctant	44	55	40

Note: The three groups differed in amount of prior, non-parental care; none of the other demographic variables was significant. [a]The standard deviation for continuous variables is shown in parentheses. [b]Amount of Prior, Non-Parental Care and Stability of Prior Non-Parental care are factors from a principal components factor analysis. [c]The Family Social Status Index is based upon Hollingshead's Four Factor Index of Social Status (1975). The range varies from 8 for very low to 66 for very high social status.

children in family day care who, in turn, had received more than the non-day care group.

Of the 224 children in the sample, 165 or 75 percent were available for testing at Posttest II. They included 32 children in CDC, 32 in FDC, and 80 of the PC group. (Five of the CDC children had changed day care centers, while 17 FDC children had switched FDC arrangements at least once between Pretesting and Posttest II.) In addition, 17 children were tested who had changed from CDC to FDC or from FDC to CDC sometime before Posttest II. These 17 children were not included in the main group comparison at Posttest II, but were set aside for the stable vs. unstable day care comparison to be described later. Lastly, 4 children in the Parent Care group were tested, but were excluded from the analysis because they had begun day care.

Table 3.2 presents a demographic comparison of the main child care groups at Posttest II. As was true at the first post-testing, the groups were significantly different from one another on only one of the 12 demographic variables, amount of prior, non-parental care ($F[2,14]=10.20$, $p<.001$). The pattern of group means was identical to that at Posttest I, with CDC children experiencing more prior care than FDC children who had experienced more care than PC children.

A comparison of Tables 3.1 and 3.2 reveals that of the children lost through attrition between first and second Post-testing, a disproportionate percentage were from ethnic minority, lower socioeconomic status, and one-parent families. The sample at Posttest II, therefore, tended to be comprised of more children from white, middle-class, and two-parent families than did the Posttest I sample.

The Posttest II sample included 39 children who changed day care arrangements at least once between Pretest and Post-test II and 42 children who remained in the initial day care placement during the same time period. These groups formed our "Unstable" and "Stable Day Care" groups, respectively. There were no significant differences between the two groups on any of the 12 demographic variables, although there was a trend for mothers of the Unstable Day Care group to have slightly more years of schooling than mothers of the Stable Day Care group ($F[1,90]=3.72$, $p<.10$).

RECRUITMENT PROCEDURES

In an effort to obtain the most representative sample of children beginning day care for the first time, we employed a

Table 3.2 Demographics of Sample at Posttest II

	Center Day Care (N=32)	Family Day Care (N=32)	Parent Care (N=80)
Pretest Age	17.90	16.60	17.60
in Months[a]	(3.27)	(3.39)	(3.78)
Sex			
Percent Male	56	53	47
Percent Female	44	47	53
Ethnicity			
Percent Black	6	7	13
Percent White	81	84	80
Percent Hispanic	10	9	6
Percent Other	3	0	1
Amount of Prior,	.52	.02	-.36
Non-Parental Care[b]	(1.31)	(.93)	(.73)
Stability Of Prior,	-.12	.29	.02
Non-Parental Care	(.88)	(1.16)	(.97)
Birth Order			
Percent First Born	62	47	61
Percent Later Born	38	53	39
Number of Siblings Present in Home			
Percent with no Sibs	59	47	57
Percent with 1 to 2 Sibs	22	41	33
Percent with $\geq$ 3 Sibs	19	12	10
Family Social	41.20	38.00	41.70
Status Index[c]	(10.96)	(13.69)	(15.04)
Family Composition			
Percent Intact	69	72	85
Percent Non-Intact	31	28	15
Maternal Age	26.30	26.90	25.50
at Parturition	(5.33)	(3.63)	(4.62)
Maternal Years	13.40	13.70	13.80
of Schooling	(2.08)	(1.90)	(1.87)
Maternal Attitude toward Day Care			
Percent Willing	50	53	56
Percent Reluctant	50	47	44

Note: The three groups differed in amount of prior, non-parental care; none of the other demographic variables were significant. [a]The standard deviation for continuous variables is shown in parenthesis. [b]Amount of Prior, Non-Parental Care and Stability of Prior, Non-Parental Care are factors from a principal components factor analysis. [c]The Family Social Status Index is based upon Hollingshead's Four Factor Index of Social Status (1975). The range varies from 8 for very low to 66 for very high social status.

wide range of recruitment procedures. These procedures included:

1. Phoning parents of all 12 to 24 month-old children on the waiting lists of 16 infant-toddler centers in the Stanford area. (These waiting lists were updated weekly.)
2. Phoning parents of 12- to 24-month olds seeking day care referrals from community coordinated child care associations and neighborhood family day care associations.
3. Mailing notices about our study to 25,000+ families receiving AFDC (Aid to Families with Dependent Children) in the two adjacent counties.
4. Mailing notices to 2,000 families whose names we obtained from the "Birth Announcements" columns of local newspapers.
5. Posting notices printed in English and Spanish in hundreds of medical clinics and physician offices, churches, laundromats, markets, beauty salons, and toy stores in the two adjacent counties.
6. Placing advertisements in the major newspapers in the area.
7. Placing radio announcements on three local radio stations.

The children in the home-reared comparison group were recruited from many of the same sources so that they would represent, as closely as possible, the same general population as our day care sample. In addition, 15 to 20 percent of the Parent Care group were initially recruited for one of the two day care groups, but never began day care and so were added to the Parent Care group.

SAMPLE OF DAY CARE CENTERS
AND FAMILY DAY CARE HOMES

The sample of day care centers included 16 of the 19 facilities in the San Francisco Peninsula area providing care for children in our age range. Not included were two centers serving school-age mothers and their children, and one center whose director declined to participate. The centers served from 12 to 100 children each (including children outside our age range), and had adult-child ratios between 1:2 and 1:13. The following is a breakdown of the type of centers represented:

Type of Center	Number Included
Private, proprietary	3
Private, non-proprietary	2

Publicly supported, community- based	5
Publicly supported, in public housing development	1
Parent co-ops, on college or university campus	4
Federally supported, on military base	1

The sample of family day care homes included 45 homes located in the same geographic area as our sample of day care centers. Approximately 30 percent of the homes were licensed, 65 percent unlicensed, and 5 percent belonged to formal family day care networks. Family day care providers were identified and asked to participate in the study when a child we had already recruited was about to begin day care in their homes. The day care homes provided for 1 to 10 children and had adult-child ratios of between 1:1 and 1:7.

PROCEDURES AND MEASURES

Measures of socialization behavior were taken during the "Play Session" at Pretesting and Posttest I and during the "Party Session" at Posttest II. The Play Session was an hour-long, standardized laboratory procedure consisting of three parts. During the initial phase, a friendly young woman whom the child had met ten minutes earlier attempted to involve the child in a standardized sequence of tasks such as ball toss and finger games. The tasks were designed to enable us to observe the child's responsiveness, cooperation, and compliance toward the adult playmate. The mother was present and accessible to the child for the entire session but, for much of the time, she sat behind a screen so that she was not readily visible.

The second part of the Play Session was designed to measure the child's reaction to frustration. The child was presented with attractive toys for a few minutes of play. The mother was then signalled to take the toys away from the child and to lock them in a cupboard. The doors of the cupboard were transparent so the child could see the toys but could not retrieve them. After five minutes (or less if the child became unduly distressed), the toys were returned to the child and the third part of the session, a period of mother-child free play began. At the end of this play period, the mother directed the child to pick up the toys.

The Party Session was a 90 minute standardized laboratory
procedure with many similarities to the Play Session. Part one
consisted of a lengthy period of free and structured play
between mother and child which enabled us to observe several
aspects of the mother-child relationship including compliance
to the mother's commands. Next, the adult playmate, a friendly
young woman whom the child had not yet met, entered the room
and attempted to involve the child in a series of standardized
tasks similar to those used in the Play Session. As in the Play
Session, the child's mother was accessible though not visible
during this interaction. This episode was followed by a juice
and cookie party for the mother, child, and adult playmate
during which there were opportunities to observe the child's
willingness both to help and to share with the adult playmate.
Finally, after a brief intermission, the child was introduced
to a series of four problem solving tasks adopted from Matas,
Arend, and Sroufe (1978). Each of the tasks required the
child to use a tool (e.g., a lever) to reach an otherwise un-
obtainable toy. Two of the tasks were administered by the adult
playmate and two by the mother. The child first attempted to
solve the problems without assistance. Prompts were later given
if the child had difficulty. The four tasks were used to observe
the child's problem solving effectiveness, persistence, task
enthusiasm, and one aspect of self-control—the use of self-
regulatory speech.

The sessions were videotaped through a one-way mirror
and scored by coders who were unaware of each child's group
membership. A brief description of the 12 "outcome" variables
is present in Table 3.3. Pearson correlations of intercoder
agreement ranged from .83 to 1.00 with a median of .90 for all
variables except compliance to the adult playmate's prohibition
at Posttest II, which had coefficients in the mid 60's.

SUMMARY OF ANALYSIS TECHNIQUES

Multiple regression procedures were used to examine the
impact of day care on the child outcome variables under study
and the possible interaction between type of care and maternal
attitude toward day care or the child's age, gender, etc. We
chose multiple regression because it is one of the few statistical
techniques which will accommodate (a) a number of independent
variables and their interactions, (b) continuous as well as
categorical independent variables, and (c) unequal cell sizes.

Table 3.3 "Outcome" Variables

Variable Name	Time Measured	Description
Social Responsiveness toward Adult Play-mate (PM)	Pretest, Posttest I, Posttest II	Child's willingness to interact with adult playmate during a series of playmate-initiated "games".
Cooperation with Adult PM	Pretest, Posttest I, Posttest II	Child's willingness to cooperate with adult playmate in a series of playmate-initiated "games", including ball toss, block building, and looking at a picture book.
Compliance to PM's Directive	Pretest, Posttest I, Posttest II	Child's compliance with requests to clean up or put away toys with which he/she had been playing.
Compliance to PM's Prohibition	Pretest, Posttest I, Posttest II	During Pretest and Posttest I, child's compliance with playmate's prohibition against child's interference in her solitary play with an attractive toy. During Posttest II, child's compliance with playmate's specific prohibitions against playing with a set of highly attractive toys.
Compliance to Mother's (M) Directive	Pretest, Posttest I	Child's compliance with requests to clean up or put away toys with which he/she had been playing

Measure	Timing	Description
Compliance to M's Prohibition	Posttest II	With surveillance: child's compliance with mother's specific prohibitions against playing with a set of highly attractive toys, in the presence of mother. Without surveillance: same as above but in absence of mother.
Distress During Frustration	Pretest, Posttest I	Child's level of distress when attractive toys with which he/she had been playing were arbitrarily locked up in a transparent cabinet.
Willingness to Help	Posttest II	Child's response to the playmate's clumsily dropping a tray of cups and to her request for help.
Willingness to Share	Posttest II	Child's response during a "party" situation in which there were not enough cookies and juice for both the child and playmate.
Problem Solving Effectiveness	Posttest II	Total amount of time required to solve the problem tasks.
Persistence	Posttest II	Percentage of time child actually spent focused on solving tasks.
Enthusiasm	Posttest II	Child's level of interest and enthusiasm during the problem solving tasks.
Self-Regulatory Speech	Posttest II	Child's use of private, egocentric, on-task speech during problem solving tasks.

The regression analysis at Posttest I included eight independent or predictor variables: Type of care (Center Day care, Family Day Care, and Parent Care), maternal attitude toward day care (willing vs. reluctant), age at pretest, gender, family intactness (father home vs. father absent), amount of prior, non-parental care, stability of prior, non-parental care, and pretest score. We used two orthogonal contrasts to code the group variable: (1) CDC, FDC vs. PC; (2) CDC vs. FDC. Dummy codes were used for maternal attitude, family intactness, and gender. Age, amount and stability of prior care, and pretest were entered as continuous variables. In addition, the following interactions between type of care and individual child or maternal characteristics were included in the regression: type of care × maternal attitude, type of care × age, type of care × gender, type of care × family intactness, type of care × amount of prior, non-parental care, type of care × stability of prior, non-parental care, and type of care × pretest score.

The specific multiple regression method used was a step-down or backward elimination procedure with two steps. In step 1, the main effects and seven interactions were entered simultaneously into the regression equation. Next, a two-stage selection process was used to reduce the number of interactions entering the equation in step 2. First, the overall F statistic for the interactions as a composite was computed. If this F did not reach marginal statistical significance ($p < .10$), the interactions were considered to contribute minimally to the regression model and were all dropped from the equation. In this way, the probability of a Type I error was set at .10 instead of .35 (.05 × 7 interactions) for the entire set of seven interactions. When the overall F did reach statistical significance, the F statistics of the individual interactions were examined. Individual interactions which did not achieve a pre-specified level of significance ($p < .15$) were considered to contribute minimally to the model and were also dropped from the equation (i.e., they were pooled into the residual term).

In the second step, the original set of main effects and only those interactions achieving the minimal level of significance were included in the regression equation. Again, F statistics were computed to test each main effect and each remaining interaction's unique contribution to predicting the dependent variable. The F statistics from this second and final step will be used in all subsequent discussions. Only significant effects of type of care, maternal attitude toward day care, and the various interactions with type of care will be discussed. The other main effects (e.g., age and gender) were included in the

regression only as control variables or covariates and will not
be considered further.

Multiple regression procedures are considered to be inappropriate for dependent variables which are either highly
skewed or which have a limited number of distinct values (e.g.,
a four-point scale). In such cases, we used logistical regression
procedures which share a number of similarities with multiple
regression. The major difference is that logistical analysis
does not require an assumption of normality. Rather, the
dependent variable is presumed to have a dichotomous distribution and must be entered in that form. For the purpose of this
analysis, non-normal dependent variables were therefore divided
at the median into "low" and "high" levels. In most other
respects, the logistical regression duplicated the original multiple
regression.

At Posttest II, the smaller sample available for analysis
necessitated a less complicated regression model. As a result,
the multiple and logistical regressions at Posttest II included
the seven predictor variables listed earlier and only the type
of care × maternal attitude interaction. As in the case of the
Posttest I analysis, we used a step-down regression procedure.

The comparison of the Stable vs. Unstable Day Care groups
at Posttest II required an even simpler regression model. Again,
either a multiple or a logistical regression was used, depending
upon the characteristics of the given dependent variable. In
either case, the model included day care stability (stable vs.
unstable), maternal day care attitude (willing vs. reluctant),
and maternal years of schooling (coded as a continuous variable)
as predictor variables or main effects. Day care stability ×
maternal attitude was included as the only interaction. No
stepping was performed; the three independent variables and
the single interaction were forced into the regression equation
on the first and only step. Maternal years of schooling was
included as a covariate to control for the somewhat higher
level of maternal education found in the Unstable Day Care
group relative to the Stable Day Care group.

GROUP AND ATTITUDE COMPARISON
AT PRETESTING

The first step in the analysis was to determine whether
children in the three child care groups displayed similar socialization behavior prior to day care entry. Also of interest was
the question of whether pretest behavior was related to maternal

attitude toward day care. To address these issues, a two-way
analysis of variance (with type of care and maternal attitude
as factors) was performed on each pretest socialization score.
In spite of the significant childrearing group differences on
amount of non-parental care reported earlier, the pretest behavior of children about to enter day care and those continuing
at home was very comparable. None of the seven pretest
measures even approached significance. Thus, the three childrearing groups were similar to one another in their socialization
behavior before day care entry.

Similarly, children in the two day care attitude groups
(collapsed over day care/parent care groups) did not differ
significantly in their behavior at pretesting. There were,
however, two non-significant trends: children whose mothers
held willing attitudes toward day care were more responsive
to the adult playmate (F $[2,210] = 2.9$, p < .10) and were somewhat less distressed during frustration ($X^2[1] = 3.7$, p < .10).
These findings at first suggest slightly more mature behavior
among children whose mothers feel confident in day care. However, this interpretation must be tempered somewhat by a
significant childrearing group × maternal attitude interaction
for social responsiveness and a similar, though non-significant
interaction for cooperation with the adult playmate. As can
be seen in Table 3.4, among children who were about to begin

Table 3.4 Significant Type of Care × Day Care Attitude Interactions at Pretest

Day Care Attitude	Center Day Care	Family Day Care	Parent Care	F
Social Responsiveness				
Willing	.77	.78	.68	$F(2,210) = 3.69$[a]
Reluctant	.65	.67	.71	
Cooperation with Adult Playmate				
Willing	.74	.72	.69	$F(2,210) = 2.89$[b]
Reluctant	.67	.71	.71	

[a]p < .05   [b]p < .10

day care, those whose mothers were comfortable with the decision to use day care were more willing to interact with the playmate and tended to be more cooperative with her than were children whose mothers were reluctant to use day care. Among children who were not beginning day care, the opposite was true: children whose mothers were negatively disposed toward day care were more responsive and cooperative with the playmate. The general thrust of these findings is consistent with Hock's (1980) observations of the mother-infant relationship of working and non-working mothers. Hock found that mothers whose beliefs about the importance of exclusive maternal care conflicted with their work status had infants who were more likely to exhibit negative reunion behavior toward their mothers indicative of insecure attachment. There is therefore growing evidence that congruence between attitudes toward exclusive maternal care and the actual use of day care may be a critical factor mediating effective parenting.

IMPACT OF DAY CARE EXPERIENCE
ON EARLY SOCIALIZATION

Table 3.5 provides the results of the comparisons of the three child-rearing groups. There was only one significant group difference at first posttest: Day care children were more socially responsive to the adult playmate than were parent care children. There was also a trend for day care children to be more cooperative with the playmate than were parent care children. This was true regardless of whether the day care children had been enrolled in center or family-based care. The day care children were no more likely to disobey either their own mothers or the experimenter and thus were no more resistent to adult authority. Rather, perhaps because of their broad range of experience with adults, CDC and FDC children were more willing to interact with an unfamiliar adult while the children reared at home tended to shy away from her.

After ten months of day care, this difference in responsiveness had disappeared. As Table 3.6 shows, the day care children were not significantly more responsive to the adult playmate than were the PC children. Table 3.6 also provides a comparison of the three child-rearing groups on the other measures of adult-orientation at Posttest II. We found little effect of either center or family day care on compliance to the mother either with or without the mother's surveillance. Nor were there reliable group differences in compliance or coopera-

Table 3.5 Mean Socialization Scores for Center Day Care, Family Day Care, and Parent Care Groups at Posttest I

Variable	Center Day Care	Family Day Care	Parent Care	F/X^2
Social Responsiveness	.77	.73	.66	$F(2,208) = 7.64$[a]
Cooperation with Playmate	.72	.71	.67	$F(2,201) = 2.6$[b]
Compliance to Playmate's Directive	.19	.27	.20	$X^2(2) < 1$
Compliance to Playmate's Prohibition	.51	.59	.50	$X^2(2) < 1$
Compliance to Mother's Directive	.63	.51	.48	$X^2(2) = 3.67$
Distress during Frustration	.52	.40	.41	$X^2(2) = 1.73$

[a] $p < .001$ [b] $p < .10$

Table 3.6 Mean Adult-Orientation Scores for Center Day Care, Family Day Care, and Parent Care Groups at Posttest II

Variable	Center Day Care	Family Day Care	Parent Care	F/X^2
Social Responsiveness	.75	.65	.66	$F(2,130) = 2.01$
Cooperation with Adult Playmate	.55	.47	.49	$F(2,141) < 1$
Compliance to Playmate's Directive	.34	.22	.39	$X^2(2) = 1.03$
Compliance to Playmate's Prohibition	.48	.47	.68	$X^2(2) = 1.26$
Compliance to Mother's Prohibition with Surveillance	.47	.47	.40	$X^2(2) < 1$
Compliance to Mother's Prohibition without Surveillance	.69	.53	.59	$X^2(2) < 1$
Willingness to Help	.66	.75	.61	$X^2(2) = 4.16$
Willingness to Share	.34	.38	.47	$X^2(2) = 8.03^a$

[a]$p < .05$

83

tion with the adult playmate. However, there was a significant difference in the degree to which children in the three groups were willing to share their snack with the adult playmate. While 47 percent of the PC children were willing to share either spontaneously or when requested to do so, only 34 percent of CDC children and 36 percent of those in FDC were willing to share. The day care children were thus more willing to risk the disapproval of both the adult playmate and their mother— even though the playmate's request to share was a "reasonable" one because there were not enough cookies and juice to go around. The day care children had apparently learned to protect their own interests, perhaps not trusting that the adults around them would adequately provide for the children's wants and needs. One can speculate that such an attitude may be adaptive in a group setting and may be a fairly accurate reflection of reality, given the number of children competing for limited resources. However, degree of sharing does not seem to be influenced by group size as CDC and FDC children were equally unlikely to share.

Table 3.7 presents a comparison of the three childrearing groups on the measures of task-orientation after ten months of day care. Note that separate scores are given for the tasks performed with the examiner and those performed with the mother. In neither case do any of the group comparisons even approach significance. Day care and parent care children were observed to be similar in their problem solving approach and effectiveness. They did not differ in the degree of persistence or enthusiasm they displayed, their use of self-regulatory speech to control their behavior, or in the length of time required to complete the tasks.

THE MEDIATING ROLE OF MATERNAL ATTITUDE
TOWARD DAY CARE

Table 3.8 offers a comparison of the two day care attitude subgroups at Posttest I. Children whose mothers expressed a "willing" attitude toward day care were less cooperative with the adult playmate than those whose mothers had a "reluctant" attitude toward day care. This was true regardless of whether the child was actually in day care. The two attitude groups did not differ on any of the other measures, but there was a significant type of care × maternal attitude interaction for response to frustration. As shown in Table 3.9, children in day care whose mothers were apprehensive about day care were

Table 3.7 Mean Task-Orientation Scores for Center Day Care, Family Day Care, and Parent Care Groups at Posttest II

Variable	Center Day Care	Family Day Care	Parent Care	F/X^2
Tasks with Experimenter				
Problem Solving				
Effectiveness	9.00	0.80	9.80	$F(1,131) = 1.65$
Persistence	.72	.73	.71	$F(1,131) < 1$
Enthusiasm	2.80	2.80	2.70	$F(1,131) < 1$
Self-Regulatory				
Speech	.55	.59	.48	$X^2(2) < 1$
Tasks with Mother				
Problem Solving				
Effectiveness	11.40	12.90	12.30	$F(1,129) < 1$
Persistence	.68	.67	.68	$F(1,131) < 1$
Enthusiasm	2.60	2.60	2.70	$F(1,131) < 1$
Self-Regulatory				
Speech	.39	.41	.44	$X^2(2) = 1.71$

Note: None of the group comparisons was significant.

Table 3.8 Mean Socialization Scores for Willing and Reluctant Day Care Attitude Groups at Posttest I

Variable	Willing Attitude	Reluctant Attitude	F/X^2
Social Responsiveness	.69	.73	$F(1,208) = 1.65$
Cooperation with			
Adult Playmate	.67	.72	$F(1,213) = 6.26$[a]
Compliance to Play-			
mate's Directive	.25	.19	$X^2(1) < 1$
Compliance to Play-			
mate's Prohibition	.50	.57	$X^2(1) < 1$
Compliance to Mother's			
Directive	.56	.48	$X^2(1) = 2.6$
Distress during			
Frustration	.42	.44	$X^2(1) < 1$

[a] $p < .01$

85

Table 3.9 Significant Type of Care × Day Care Attitude Interaction for Distress during Frustration at Posttest I

Day Care Attitude	Center Day Care	Family Day Care	Parent Care	Significant Contrast	X^2 for Contrast
Willing	.40	.33	.47	CDC, FDC vs PC	$X^2(1) = 5.08$[a]
Reluctant	.67	.44	.30		

[a]$p < .05$

86

more upset when confronted with a frustrating situation than children whose mothers were comfortable with day care. Among non-day care children, the opposite effect was found: Children whose mothers had willing attitudes toward day care cried more when frustrated. In other words, children whose mothers' actual decision whether to use day care was incongruent with their attitude toward day care were less tolerant of frustration than children whose mothers' behavior and attitudes were congruent.

We have seen this pattern of findings on more than one occasion in this study. As reported earlier, at Pretest, children whose mothers' attitude toward day care was inconsistent with their use of day care were less socially responsive and tended to be less cooperative with an unfamiliar, though friendly adult. At Posttest I, children in the discrepant maternal attitude group (regardless of whether they were enrolled in day care) also took longer to calm down after separation in the Strange Situation (Everson, 1981) and were less compliant to their mothers in a free play activity (Sarnat, 1982). These results suggest that mothers who are in conflict over their decision to work outside the home or to remain at home with their children may have children who are less well adjusted. However, no similar pattern of findings was observed at Posttest II. Either the role conflict was transitory or mothers with the most intense feelings acted to resolve their conflict by enrolling their children in, or removing their children from, day care sometime before Posttest II.

How maternal role dissatisfaction actually translates into changes in the mother-child relationship is a matter of speculation. It is not difficult to imagine, however, that maternal guilt, dissatisfaction, or resentment could lead to low morale, thereby decreasing parenting effectiveness at least temporarily. In support of this interpretation, Sarnat (1982) found that mothers in the discrepant day care attitude group were more likely to become angry and impatient when issuing commands to their children than were mothers whose attitudes and behavior toward day care were consistent.

At Posttest II, day care attitude followed a very different pattern. There were significant or nearly-significant differences between children whose mothers were positively disposed toward day care and those who were negatively disposed toward day care on 8 of the 16 measures of socialization. As can be seen in Table 3.10, children whose mothers had "willing" day care attitudes were less cooperative with the adult playmate, less willing to share with her, and less likely (although not quite

Table 3.10 Mean Adult-Orientation Scores for Willing and Reluctant Day Care Attitude Groups at Posttest II

Variable	Willing Attitude	Reluctant Attitude	F/X^2
Social Responsiveness	.65	.71	$F(1,130) = 2.13$
Cooperation with Adult Playmate	.46	.53	$F(1,140) = 6.31^a$
Compliance to Playmate's Directive	.35	.23	$X^2(1) < 1$
Compliance to Playmate's Prohibition	.60	.58	$X^2(1) < 1$
Compliance to Mother's Prohibition with Surveillance	.33	.54	$X^2(1) = 4.80^a$
Compliance to Mother's Prohibition without Surveillance	.59	.61	$X^2(1) < 1$
Willingness to Help	.57	.74	$X^2(1) = 3.49^b$
Willingness to Share	.27	.60	$X^2(1) = 16.9^c$

[a]$p < .05$ [b]$p < .10$ [c]$p < .001$

significantly so) to help her. They were also much less likely
to comply with their mother's prohibitions against playing with
certain toys than were children whose mothers held negative
day care attitudes. Whether they were enrolled in day care or
not, children whose mothers were positively disposed toward
day care also displayed a markedly inferior approach to problem
solving compared tc children whose mothers were less comfortable
with day care (see Table 3.11). The problem solving approach
of the positive day care attitude group was characterized by
less persistence, enthusiasm, self-regulatory speech, and overall effectiveness in tasks with the adult playmate and less self-
regulatory speech in tasks with their mothers.* Maternal attitude
toward day care assessed at the pretesting, therefore, was
associated with a broad range of behavioral outcomes ten months
later, all of which favored children whose mothers expressed
concerns about the use of day care.

There was also evidence that maternal attitude toward day
care played a role in mediating the significant effect of day
care on sharing behavior reported earlier. As can be seen in
Table 3.12, day care had virtually no effect on sharing among
children whose mothers had "reluctant" day care attitudes.
The means for the reluctant day care attitude subgroup were
nearly identical across the three childrearing groups. However,
children in day care whose mothers initially held positive attitudes
toward day care were much less willing to share than children
who remained home with their mothers. In fact, among children
in the positive day care attitude group, only 6 percent of those
in center day care and 13 percent of those in family day care
were willing to share compared with 39 percent of those who
did not enter day care. Although this type of care × day care
attitude interaction did not quite reach traditionally accepted
levels of significance, it does suggest that children whose
mothers have positive attitudes toward day care may be especially
vulnerable to suffering negative consequences in day care. Or,
to put it another way, the specific effects of day care may depend

---

*We speculate that the day care attitude comparisons for
persistence, enthusiasm, and problem solving effectiveness,
though consistent in direction with the experimenter-presented
tasks, failed to reach statistical significance because of the
great variability in how mothers presented the tasks. The experimenters, in contrast, followed a standardized protocol which
reduced the variance of the scores.

Table 3.11 Mean Task-Orientation Scores for Willing and Reluctant Attitude Groups at Posttest II

Variable	Willing Attitude	Reluctant Attitude	F/X^2
	Tasks with Experimenter		
Problem Solving Effectiveness[a]	10.10	9.00	$F(1,129) = 6.55$[b]
Persistence	.67	.78	$F(1,131) = 10.36$[b]
Task Enthusiasm	2.60	3.00	$F(1,130) = 18.37$[c]
Self-Regulatory Speech	.40	.66	$X^2(1) = 8.14$[b]
	Tasks with Mother		
Problem Solving Effectiveness[a]	12.60	11.80	$F(1,129) < 1$
Persistence	.67	.70	$F(1,129) < 1$
Enthusiasm	2.60	2.80	$F(1,129) = 1.65$
Self-Regulatory Speech	.35	.51	$X^2(1) = 4.10$[d]

[a]In minutes   [b]$p < .01$ [c]$p < .001$ [d]$p < .05$

Table 3.12 Significant Type of Care × Day Care Attitude Interaction for Willingness to Share at Posttest II

Day Care Attitude	Center Day Care	Family Day Care	Parent Care	X^2
Willing	.06	.13	.39	$X^2(2) = 5.03$[a]
Reluctant	.63	.59	.58	

[a]$p < .08$

in large measure on maternal attitude toward day care and other family characteristics.

This interpretation receives support from other findings of our study which suggest that day care has adverse effects on the attachment behavior of children in the "willing" but not the "reluctant" attitude subgroup (Everson et al., 1983). Specifically, after 10 months of day care, the mother-child relationship of children in the willing attitude group was marked by less closeness, harmony, and mutual enjoyment in comparison to children cared for at home by their mothers.

A question yet to be addressed is how does maternal attitude toward day care account for these findings? In what ways do mothers with "willing" attitudes toward day care differ from those with "reluctant" attitudes? One possibility we considered was that day care attitude might be confounded in our sample with another characteristic of the child or family such as amount of prior care or mother's level of education, and that the other variable, not day care attitude, accounted for our results. To test this hypothesis, we compared the willing and reluctant attitude groups on the 12 demographic variables described earlier. There were no significant differences on any of these demographic variables. If there were a confounding, it is not an obvious one.

Next, we speculated that the effects of day care attitude might be partially attributed to variations in the quality of care mothers in the two attitude groups selected for their children. Perhaps mothers who had few concerns about the influence of day care on their children were less careful in selecting quality arrangements than mothers who felt apprehensive about using out-of-home care. We therefore compared day care children in the two attitude groups on a number of indices of day care quality including adult-child ratio, percentage of time spent interacting with adults, and adult responsiveness to child bids. Again, there were no significant differences between children in the two day care attitude groups.

At this point, our speculation has taken the following form. We hypothesize that attitude toward day care subsumes a number of beliefs and attitudes toward childrearing which reflect the mother's feelings of closeness for her toddler and her personal and emotional commitment to her child. As a result, attitude toward day care can probably be considered a gross index of the degree of closeness of the mother-child relationship. Mothers who are reluctant to leave their toddlers in day care thus are likely to have closer, more intense relationships with their children than do mothers with a more relaxed view of day care.

As a result, we believe that mothers who are apprehensive about using day care may be more effective socializers of their children. First, mothers with close relationships with their children are likely to spend more time interacting with them. If these mothers do send their children to day care, they may also be more likely to attempt to compensate for the time apart with extra quality time during the evenings and weekends. Second, mothers with close relationships with their children are likely to be more emotionally invested in them and to see their child's behavior as a personal reflection on them. Consequently, such mothers are likely to set higher behavioral standards for their children and are more likely to enforce those standards. In support of this argument, mothers in the reluctant day care attitude group in our sample were observed to monitor the behavior of their children more intently during the pretest home visit than did mothers who were positively disposed toward day care (Everson et al., 1983). Third, mothers with more intense relationships with their toddlers are likely to view their own parenting role as critical and irreplaceable and are therefore less likely to relinquish their socializing responsibility to others. Finally, because of the strong affective bond between mother and child, the child may be more likely to internalize the mother's values and standards for behavior.

THE MEDIATING ROLE OF OTHER
CHILD CHARACTERISTICS

In addition to maternal attitude toward day care, we were also interested in examining the role of four characteristics of the child in mediating the impact of day care on early socialization. These characteristics included: age at day care entry, gender, and the amount and stability of prior, non-parental care. With the exceptions of a few isolated findings, there were no significant interactions between childrearing group and any of these child characteristics. Consequently, the effect of day care did not depend, to any meaningful degree, on the child's age, gender, or prior separation experience. We were particularly surprised that amount of prior, non-parental care was not important in mediating the impact of day care, given the range of separation experience represented in our sample. Some of the children in our sample had literally never been away from one parent or the other before beginning day care, while other children had experienced substituted care for 90 or more hours per month since birth.

Before interpreting these findings, a word of caution is in order. We were only able to examine the mediating role of these child characteristics at Posttest I. Because of the reduced sample available at Posttest II, we did not examine the interaction of type of care with these four child characteristics. It is possible, therefore, that the role of age, gender, etc. in mediating the specific impact of day care might not become apparent until after the first five months of day care.

THE EFFECT OF STABLE VS. UNSTABLE CARE

In order to assess the effect of unstable care on early socialization we compared 39 children who had changed day care arrangements at least once in the first ten months of day care with 42 children who remained in the same setting during this time. The children in the Unstable Day Care group had changed arrangements from 1 to 3 times with a mean of 1.2 times. There were no significant differences between the Stable and Unstable Day Care groups on any of the outcome measures at Posttest II. Consequently, unstable day care was not found to have an effect on socialization behavior after ten months of care.

CONCLUSION

We found few effects of either center or family day care on children beginning care as toddlers. Contrary to other studies, day care children were not observed to be less adult-oriented or less responsive to adult authority. Nor did they differ from children reared exclusively at home on such aspects of task-orientation as persistence, enthusiasm, and the use of self-regulatory speech to control their own behavior. It is possible that the behavioral consequences of day care reported by others are seen only after more extended periods of time in group care, or that the effects are subtle and difficult to measure until later ages.

Of the two significant types of care effects we obtained, one favored the day care groups. That is, children with five months of day care experience were more responsive to the unfamiliar examiner than were home-reared children, though this difference had disappeared by the second posttesting. Our finding that children in day care were less willing to share with an adult playmate than children cared for by their mothers may be a precursor to the reduced interest in pleasing adults and

the lower levels of prosocial behavior often reported among children with more extensive day care experience. A close examination of the subgroup means, however, reveals that unwillingness
to share is not common among all children in our day care sample.
Rather, the effect is mediated by maternal attitude toward day
care. In fact, maternal attitude toward day care measured at
pretesting predicted a wide range of behaviors ten months later
at Posttest II. This was true regardless of whether the child
actually ever entered day care.

It is particularly intriguing that our findings for maternal
attitude toward day care closely parallel the findings of others
for the effects of day care. We observed less cooperation, compliance, persistence, and prosocial behavior among children
whose mothers had initially expressed no reluctance to use day
care—just as other investigators have found less cooperation,
compliance, persistence, and prosocial behavior among children
with extensive day care histories. This similarity raises the
question of whether at least some of the inappropriate socialization
behavior thought to result from day care may actually be related
to differences in maternal attitudes (or the mother-child relationship) that predate day care entry. Presumably, mothers who
have the fewest concerns about using day care are precisely
the ones who are likely to enroll their children in group care,
at an early age, for extended periods of time.

In conclusion, these findings offer evidence that day care
per se may exert a less substantial influence on the process of
socialization than is often believed. The course of socialization
is probably determined more by the child's interactions with
his/her mother and other family members than by whether the
child attends day care. Forty hours a week in a day care
center does not alter the fact that the family is the young
child's prime socializing agent. As a result, if one wants to
understand the child's response to adult authority, degree of
impulse control, or quality of work-related habits, one may
need to look no further than the child's front door.

REFERENCES

Ainsworth, M. D. S., Blehar, M. C., Waters, E., and Wall, S.
Patterns of attachment: A psychological study of the strange
situation. New York, NY: John Wiley & Sons, 1978.

Anderson, C. W. Attachment in daily separations: Reconceptualizing day care and maternal employment issues. Child Development, 1980, 51, 242-245.

Barton, M. and Schwarz, C. Day care in the middle class: Effects in elementary school. Paper presented at the American Psychological Association Annual Convention, Los Angeles, August 1981.

Belsky, J. and Steinberg, L. D. The effects of day care: A critical review. Child Development, 1978, 49, 929-949.

Clarke-Stewart, A. Day care: A new context for research and development. In M. Perlmutter (Ed.), The Minnesota Symposium on Child Psychology, Vol. 17, Hillsdale, NJ: Lawrence Erlbaum Assoc., 1983.

Cronbach, L. J. and Snow, R. E. Aptitudes and instructional methods: A handbook for research on interactions. New York: Irvington Publishers, 1977.

Everson, M. D., Sarnat, L., Kermoian, R., and Ambron, S. R. Day care and attachment behavior: The mediating role of maternal attitude. Unpublished manuscript. Stanford University, 1983.

Everson, M. D. The impact of day care on the attachment behavior of 12 to 24 month olds. Unpublished doctoral dissertation, Stanford University, 1981.

Golden, M., Rosenbluth, L., Grossi, M. T., Policave, H. J., Freeman, H., Jr., and Brownless, M. The New York City infant day care study: A comparative study of licensed group and family day care programs and the effects of these programs on children and their families. New York, NY: Medical and Health Research Association of New York City, Inc., 1978.

Gunnarson, L. Children in day care and family care in Sweden: A follow-up. Bulletin No. 21, Department of Educational Research, University of Gothenburg, Sweden, 1978.

Hock, E. Working and non-working mothers and their infants: A comparative study of maternal caregiving characteristics and infant social behavior. Merrill-Palmer Quarterly of Behavior and Development, 1980, 26, 79-101.

Hock, E. Working and non-working mothers with infants: Perceptions of their careers, their infants' needs, and

satisfaction with mothering. Developmental Psychology,
1978, 14, 37-43.

Hoffman, L. W. Effects of maternal employment on the child—
a review of the research. Developmental Psychology, 1974,
10, 204-228.

Hollingshead, A. B. Four-factor index of social status. Unpublished manuscript. Yale University, 1975.

Kagan, J., Kearsley, R. B., and Zelazo, P. R. Infancy: Its
place in human development. Cambridge: Harvard University
Press, 1978.

Kardiner, Abram. The individual and his society: The psycho-
dynamics of primitive social organization. New York, NY:
Columbia University Press, 1947.

Lamb, M. E. Qualitative Aspects of Mother and Father Infant
Attachments. Infant Behavior and Development, 1978, 1,
265-275.

Lamb, M. E., Owen, M. T., and Chase-Lansdale, L. The
working in the intact family. In Abidin, R. R. (Ed.), Handbook of parent education, Illinois: Charles S. Thomas,
Publishers, 1979.

Lippman, M. Z. and Grote, B. H. Social-emotional effects of
day care. Final Project Report. Washington, D.C. Office
of Child Development, 1974. (ERIC Document Reproduction
Service No. EC110164.)

Macrae, J. W. and Herbert-Jackson, E. Are behavioral effects
of infant day care programs specific? Developmental Psychology, 1975, 12, 269-270.

Matas, L., Arend, R. A., and Sroufe, L. A. Continuity of
adaptation in the second year: The relationship between
quality of attachment and later competence. Child Development, 1978, 547-556.

Robertson, A. Day care and children's responsiveness to
adults. In E. Zigler and E. W. Gordon (Eds.), Day care:
Scientific and social policy issues. Boston, MA: Auburn
House Publishing, 1982.

Roopnarine, J. L. and Lamb, M. E. The effects of day care
on attachment and exploratory behavior in a strange situation.
Merrill-Palmer Quarterly of Behavior and Development, 1978,
24, 85-95.

Roopnarine, J. L. and Lamb, M. E. Peer and parent-child
interaction before and after enrollment in nursery school.
Journal of Applied Developmental Psychology, 1980, 1, 77-81.

Rubenstein, J., Howes, C., and Boyle, P. A two year follow-up
of infants in community-based day care. Journal of Child
Psychology and Psychiatry, 1981, 22, No. 3, 209-218.

Rutter, M. Maternal deprivation, 1972-1978: New findings,
new concepts, new approaches. Child Development, 1979,
50, 283-305.

Sarnat, L. Z. Variations in care: Effects of child compliance
and maternal control. Unpublished doctoral dissertation,
Stanford University, 1982.

Schwarz, J. C. Effects of group day care in the first two
years. Paper presented at the Biennial Meeting of the
Society for Research in Child Development. Detroit, MI,
April 1983.

Schwarz, J. C., Strickland, R. G., and Krolick, G. Infant
day care: Effects at preschool age. Developmental Psychology, 1974, 10, 502-506.

4.

Day Care Childrens' Relationships to Their Mothers and Caregivers: An Inquiry into the Conditions for the Development of Attachment

Ricardo C. Ainslie and Christine W. Anderson

A primary interest of research on day care effects has been whether or not long periods away from the mother have a deleterious effect on the mother-child relationship. Daycare research has, therefore, traditionally focused on the child's relationship to the mother. Most studies examining this question have found that children in day care continue to prefer their mothers over their caregivers. Similarly, most have concluded that the experience of day care does not necessarily have a more general detrimental effect upon the mother-child relationship (see Belsky, this volume; Belsky and Steinberg, 1979; and Rutter, 1981 for reviews).

In one example of this type of study, Farran and Ramey (1977) sought to answer the question "Does day care placement in infancy affect the developing bond between mother and child so that the child forms a stronger, alternative bond to his day

---

We wish to thank the Hogg foundation for Mental Health at the University of Texas at Austin for its generous support of this research. We also wish to thank Gemma Ainslie and Guy Manaster for their helpful comments in preparing this manuscript.

Christine Anderson died in an automobile accident when this project was in its final stages of completion. In keeping with an understanding arrived at prior to her death, the publications derived from this research have alternating first authorship.

care teacher?" (p. 1112) To evaluate this question they used
a laboratory procedure in which the child was placed in a room
where the mother, the caregiver, and a stranger were present.
The room was divided into 4 quadrants, with a pile of toys in
the center of the room. The toys were equidistant from each
of the adults' chairs. Farran and Ramey found that day care
children were significantly more likely to interact with their
mothers than with either the caregiver or stranger. In fact,
there were no significant differences in the children's interactions with the caregiver and the stranger. Further, these
day care children spent significantly more time in the mother's
quadrant (i.e. closer to mother physically) than time in the
quadrants of the other two participants. Because children who
had been in day care since infancy clearly displayed a preference for interacting and being close to their mothers rather
than to their caregivers, Farran and Ramey concluded that
there was little support for the fear that children's relationships
with their caregivers at day care might be at the expense of
children's preferences for their mothers. The authors note
that these differences in behavior were present even though
the children spent at least half of their waking time each day
with their caregivers in a pleasant, stimulating, and reinforcing
environment. Thus, they concluded that the infants were more
attached to their mothers than to their caregivers. Kagan,
Kearsley, and Zelazo (1978) reported similar results.

Such findings have reassured parents and researchers
alike that day care need not constitute a threat to the primacy
of the parent-child relationship. As Belsky (this volume) notes,
with these concerns laid to rest, day care researchers have
turned to more specific questions regarding the day care
environment and its relationship to other aspects of the day
care child's development. For example, rather than global
questions regarding whether or not caregiver-infant relationships replace the mother-infant relationship, one might ask
what is the nature of a child's relationship to the caregiver?
Are there more subtle ways in which that relationship affects
the parent-child relationship? Do day care children actually
develop an attachment to their caregivers? Is such an attachment something to be desired rather than feared?

In addition to their relevance to our understanding of the
day care experience, these questions are related to issues of
more general developmental interest. For example, developmental theorists interested in attachment have given some
attention to describing the conditions that foster secure attachment between a mother and her child (e.g. Ainsworth, 1969;

1973; Ainsworth, Bell, and Stayton, 1971; 1972). However, the literature pertaining to the possibility of multiple attachments, differences between attachment relationships, and the circumstances governing the formation of multiple attachments is relatively scant. We know comparatively little about attachment in the context of more complex social environments in which an infant is involved in sustained ways with other-than-mother adults.

The development of attachment has been discussed and assessed in a dyadic context because attachment, by definition, refers to the quality of relationship which characterizes a particular infant-adult pair. However, Bronfenbrenner's theoretical contributions (1979) underscore the limitations of this sort of an approach by alerting us to the fact that different developmental contexts—including, we might add, different primary relationships—impinge upon and affect the child's "attachment world", and hence, the child's socioemotional development. In other words, children develop in a complex social network in which a variety of relationships and events affect one another, providing a more general overarching context within which the child's psychological environment is defined. Some of the questions that such a conceptualization of child development raises are these: How many people can an infant actually become attached to? What are the necessary conditions for multiple attachments to be formed? How do attachment relationships affect each other?

While the present chapter cannot hope to answer all of these questions, it does have a direct bearing on them. Specifically, we will examine the day care child's relationship to the caregiver as an attachment figure. We will first present an overview of the attachment construct, followed by a discussion of the relevance of attachment theory to understanding the child's relationship to the caregiver in the day care setting. We will then turn to a discussion of selected studies from the day care literature which contribute to our understanding of the infant-caregiver relationship. Finally, a study comparing infants' behavior in the Strange Situation with their mothers versus with their caregivers will be presented.

THE INFANT-CAREGIVER RELATIONSHIP:
ASSUMPTIONS

In order to examine the construct of attachment (and multiple attachments) as it pertains to day care, it is necessary

to specify the sorts of day care environments under consideration, since there is considerable variation in these. The discussion in this chapter will assume day care experiences which begin
during the first year of life. Further, we are interested in day
care experiences which constitute a significant portion of a
child's daily activity. Finally, we must assume some consistency
of exposure over time to a specific caregiver.

These three conditions are important because they speak
directly to the assumptions underlying the attachment construct,
and day care research has been relatively non-specific on these
very points. For example, day care studies have sometimes
included children who varied considerably in length of time in
day care, age at which the child was enrolled in day care, and
the number of hours per day actually spent in day care. Further,
some studies have included samples of children which were very
heterogeneous in age at the time of participation in the study;
such heterogeneity confounds a number of developmental variables, since relatively small age differences in children under
five years often reflect major differences in development.
Clearly, these are important variables that directly affect what
we can conclude about day care, and about the specific characteristics and effects of the day care "experience" for a particular
child. For purposes of clarity, then, the present discussion
will assume an infant day care setting, in which a child spends
a substantial portion of each day in the presence of a caregiver
with whom the child has had ongoing contact.

Without these specifications, an examination of attachment
vis-a-vis the caregiver would be meaningless as there would
not have been sufficient opportunities for the child to actually
develop a relationship of substance with the caregiver. Further,
since attachment theorists view the first year of life as crucial
in terms of the overall development of attachment, day care
enrollment beginning in this period would presumably have the
greatest impact upon the nature and quality of attachment(s)
developed. In fact, it is for these very reasons that Rutter
(1981) has suggested that infant day care may be the most
important form of day care for researchers to consider.

ATTACHMENT

The concept of attachment has played an important role
in research regarding the impact of day care upon children's
socioemotional development. Attachment is defined as the
affectional tie between an infant and its caretaker which is

enduring over space and time (Ainsworth and Bell, 1970).
Attachment is also a mode of relating to a specific figure, with
individual differences reflecting qualitative differences in
caretaker-infant relationships. Sroufe (1979) and Sroufe and
Fleeson (1983) have argued that these differences must be
thought of in terms of "internalized" dimensions of relating,
rather than situationally determined responses. This distinction
is considered a vital one by attachment theorists, since the
notion of attachment as an "organizational construct" (Sroufe
and Waters, 1977) implies that early caretaker-infant experiences
become structured into complex patterns of behavior, expectation, and attitudes toward others. In short, the infant's history
of relationships leads to a certain stability in personality organization, with implications for subsequent socioemotional development.

Ainsworth (1972) divides the development of attachment
into three general phases. The first, taking place during the
first half of the first year, is termed the Pre-Attachment Phase.
From birth, the human infant has a repertoire of behaviors
which promote proximity and/or contact with others. Ainsworth
views these behaviors as universal, "appearing in all cultures
and following a reasonably predictable and regular schedule of
emergence in development" (p. 107). However, this phase in
development is termed the pre-attachment phase because these
behaviors are not exhibited preferentially toward particular
persons in the environment. Rather, they are indiscriminate
and nondifferential. For this reason Ainsworth believes that
one cannot actually speak of attachment to specific figures
during the earliest months of life.

The second phase is termed the phase of Attachment-In-
The-Making. Its onset is difficult to specify because the
infant is capable of discriminations through some modalities
before others. However, during this phase various proximity-
promoting behaviors—attachment behaviors—become discriminating
and differential (Ainsworth, 1972). For example, whereas in
the first months of life an infant may smile indiscriminately at
any human face, during this second phase smiling toward unfamiliar figures becomes less frequent, while smiles to the
mother "and perhaps to a few other familiar figures occur more
readily, frequently, and fully, even under conditions when
the preferred figure does not offer an optimal stimulus" (p. 108).
The end of this phase is rather clear, in Ainsworth's view, and
generally occurs in the second half of the first year of life,
"with 7 months as the milestone for many babies" (p. 107).

The third phase in the development of attachment is termed the Phase-of-Clear-Cut Attachment. This phase follows shortly after the discriminating and differential behavior of the second phase has been established, and is characterized by a great increase in active proximity-seeking behavior. Clearly, motor development plays an important role here as well, since the infant is now capable of bringing him or herself into close proximity with the attachment figure or figures. Ainsworth also notes that cognitive development is such that at this time the infant also begins to have a concept of attachment figures as existing even though they are not present to perception. "It is roughly coincident with the emergence of his ability actively to seek proximity and to conceive of absent objects as existing that a baby can be judged to have become attached to specific persons" (p. 108).

Attachment theorists often emphasize the notion that attachment constitutes or reflects a specific and unique relationship to a particular caregiver. For example, Sroufe and Fleeson (1983) describe attachment as an inner organization of behavioral systems which not only controls the "stable propensity" to seek proximity to the attachment figure, but also is responsible for the distinctive quality of the organization of specific attachment behaviors through which an individual promotes proximity with a specific attachment figure. From this vantage point, attachment is not considered a general construct, but rather, it is seen as referring to a specific relationship between the infant and a specific other. The view that attachment is specific to the child's relationship with a particular attachment figure, as opposed to being a general trait, is noted elsewhere in the attachment literature as well (e.g. Ainsworth, 1972; Ainsworth et al. 1978). Thus, one view of attachment emphasizes its uniqueness in reference to a particular relationship.

However, a child's relationship with other individuals is clearly not altogether independent of the child's relationships with primary caretakers. For example, Ainsworth (1972) notes that attachments to one or a few other figures may emerge simultaneously. In this context she states that it is plausible to expect that an attachment relationship with one figure, "especially a secure attachment", may facilitate relationships with others. "To have experienced security, trust, interest, and gratification in relations with one figure may predispose a child to expect these desiderata in relations with other figures, and the behaviors which he has come characteristically to display in interactions with an attachment figure may, when displayed in interaction with other figures, evoke behavior from them which continues to support his optimistic expectations" (p. 130, present authors' emphasis).

Other attachment theorists also emphasize the motion that a child's attachment to primary caretakers influences the quality of other relationships that the child develops. According to Sroufe and Fleeson (1983), "Relationships with peers and others formed in early childhood (and later in more complex ways) would be strongly predictable from the quality of the early primary relationships" (p. 2). They further state that: ". . . predictability (is) enhanced, by the fact that individuals select and shape each other in terms of the dispositions, inclinations, and expectancies brought from prior relationships. Individuals tend not to combine these dispositions in random fashion, but to recreate aspects of relationship systems previously experienced" (p. 2). And, finally, ". . . the infant . . . will behave according to established dyadic patterns and, in so doing, will reveal qualities of the relationship history" (p. 3).

Statements such as these emphasize a dual quality to attachment: it is seen as a unique organizer of the young child's relationship to a particular person or persons, while at the same time becoming the basis for generalization to at least some other relationships. Both of these views are applicable to the day care situation. Given full-time infant day care, the day care setting may lend itself to the development of an attachment relationship whose characteristics would be a function of the quality of the caregiver's interactions with the infant. However, the above discussion also underscores the fact that the sort of relationship that a day care child develops with its caregiver may also be related to the attachment that the child has developed to a parental figure.

In order to assess the quality of infant attachment, Ainsworth developed the Strange Situation procedure (a description of the procedure is given below). This laboratory procedure has been found to reliably distinguish three types of attachment: Anxious/Avoidant (A), Anxious/Resistant (C), and Secure (B) (e.g., Ainsworth et al., 1978). Attachment theorists have accumulated an impressive array of studies buttressing their contention that attachment is an important concept for our understanding of human development, although their contributions have not been received uncritically (e.g. Cairns, 1972; Gewirtz, 1972a; Lamb et al., 1983; Weinraub, Brooks, and Lewis, 1977). The value of this construct for developmentalists rests on two important elements. The first is the fact that the quality of infant-mother attachment has been found to be stable over time, at least for middle-class populations, despite the fact that specific attachment behaviors (such as contact seeking, amount of distress at separation, etc.) are not. For example, Waters (1978) found attachment classifications to be highly stable between eighteen and twenty-four months.

The second reason the construct of attachment is important is that a number of studies have found quality of attachment to be predictive of a variety of behaviors and capacities. For example, Matas, Arend, and Sroufe (1978) found that infants assessed as securely attached at 18 months were more "enthusiastic, persistent, cooperative, and, in general, more effective than insecurely attached infants" when assessed at two years (p. 547). Similarly, in a longitudinal study, Arend, Gove, and Sroufe (1979) found Strange Situation assessments at 18 months and competence at two years to be significantly related to "ego resiliency" and "ego control" at age 4 to 5 years.

IMPLICATIONS FOR DAY CARE

The framework of attachment theory raises important questions for our consideration of day care as a developmental context. We can begin by looking at the conditions which are required for attachment to develop. Implicit in the formulations of attachment theorists is the understanding that the human infant requires an opportunity to develop an attachment relationship, that is, time and exposure to another person. Without such an opportunity a caretaker remains at the periphery of the infant's social world, and in some respects may be more a stranger than an attachment figure. The experiences which ultimately create the basis for an infant's transition from a "pre-attachment" type of relationship, that is, one that is essentially indiscriminate, to a relationship of an "attachment-in-the-making" or a "clear-cut attachment" character, have not been clearly specified. However, it is evident that in addition to an infant's being in proximity to the caretaker, the caretaker must also be in a position to interact with the infant in ways that directly affect the infant's well being. For example, although they may be present continuously, it is assumed that young siblings do not become attachment figures for an infant.*

---

*It is not clear how one might conceptualize sibling relationships within the framework of attachment theory. Infants obviously develop relationships with close-in-age siblings and may even find their presence soothing; this is particularly evident in the case of twins as described in Ainslie, in press.

Presumably this is because siblings do not function as caregivers. That is, they do not attend to the infant's needs in ways that are vital to the infant. Thus, mere exposure to other individuals is not a sufficient basis for the infant to develop an attachment. The opportunity must be translated into a range of interactions or direct involvements with the infant. Ainsworth (1967) and Schaffer and Emerson (1964a) suggest a child's choice of attachment figure(s) is based upon the amount and nature of the interaction he experiences with each figure familiar enough to be a candidate for attachment.

In general, the actual content of these interactions is not specified by attachment theorists (except to relate more adequate and responsive mothering to secure attachments—e.g., Ainsworth et al., 1978; Grossman and Grossman, 1982). This is the case because an infant can become attached to a caretaker under many different conditions. Once a certain threshold of experiences and interactions with a caretaker which make the development of attachment possible is attained, there is a great deal of room for different kinds of attachment relationships to develop. The broad range of possible caretaker-infant interactions have implications for differences in the quality of attachment. Thus, it is important to distinguish between an infant's opportunity to develop an attachment relationship, and the kind of attachment that is developed. Infants with little exposure to a person, or infants whose contact with another is lacking in primary, substantive interactions, will not become attached to that person. Given the prerequisite experiences, however, a child will become attached to a caregiver. The quality of those experiences then becomes the basis for determining the quality (e.g. anxious/resistant, anxious/avoidant, or secure) of attachment.

With these comments in mind, it can be readily seen that the construct of attachment is directly relevant to full-time infant day care. Such experiences potentially meet all of the conditions necessary for the development of attachment relationships to their caregivers. Infants are in the care of one or two adult caregivers for a major portion of their day. In some instances, infants spend more waking hours with caregivers than they do with their parents. Further, these contacts, while perhaps not of the intensity of mother-infant interactions (and no doubt proportionately less specifically dyadic in nature), do involve important infant needs. For example, caregivers feed and change infants, and may rock or otherwise comfort them when they are in distress. In addition, free-play periods afford the opportunity for some one-to-one interactions, although it is usually the case that during these periods the caregiver is "shared" with other infants. Thus, caregivers are obvious candidates for becoming objects of attachment, whether or not this is in fact the case in any given instance.

Ainsworth provides some support for this thesis. For example, in the context of discussing the effects of distressing separations from parents, Ainsworth (1972) comments: "If substitute mother figures are available, there is no doubt that an infant or young child will avail himself of the comfort and nurturance offered by them eventually, and, in proportion to their accessibility as figures with whom he can interact, he may become attached to them" (p. 122, present authors' emphasis). While Ainsworth is referring to extended separations during which children do not have contact with their mothers, the crucial element seems to be the distress engendered by the separation from parents, and the eventual acceptance of substitute relationships to help mitigate the felt loss. Although day care does not constitute the extreme kind of separation experience which Ainsworth is addressing, entry into day care also involves long periods of separation from family members and is often a difficult and stressful experience. For example, both mothers and caregivers describe the first several weeks in day care as distressing for many infants (Ainslie and Anderson, in press).

Some of Ainsworth's observations further suggest that infants become attached to caregivers. For example, she notes that prior to the development of attachment, infants who are distressed manifest their distress in a manner which is somewhat diffuse and undirected. Further, such infants are likely to adapt themselves rather readily to mother substitutes. Infants older than 7 or 8 months, however, behave differently, according to Ainsworth (1972). Their distress is "more intense, more long-lasting, more clearly directed toward recovery of the mother figure, and not readily alleviated by attention from caregivers" (p. 112). Ainsworth is referring here to a caregiver who is essentially a stranger to the infant. However, since this kind of "separation protest" is not regularly evident in most day care children after the first few weeks in day care, the absence of such distress in older infants who are in day care could be interpreted as reflecting a degree of attachment to the caregiver.

Finally, Ainsworth (1972) cites fostering studies, such as those of the Robertsons (e.g., 1968a,b) to demonstrate that separation distress may be greatly alleviated by sensitive non-parental figures who encourage the development of an attachment relationship. She further notes that these same studies strongly suggest that such sensitive substitute care does not diminish a child's attachment to his own parents, and facilitates rather than hampers the reestablishment of harmonious and secure relations upon reunion. These observations would seem to have direct implications for the day care setting. They clearly suggest that given a necessity for day care, the potential strains engendered by long periods of separation from parental figures can be minimized by sensitive caregivers who encourage the development of an attachment relationship to themselves.

As this material indicates, the attachment literature lends support to the thesis that in some circumstances day care infants can become attached to their caregivers. It is therefore necessary to consider that this is a possibility in the context of ongoing exposure and interaction.

DAY CARE LITERATURE

There are a number of day care studies that directly address the points that have been discussed above. For example, in a study comparing private substitute care with maternal care, Rubenstein, Pedersen, and Yarrow (1977) found important differences between mothers and caregivers in the ways in which they interacted with the infant. The subjects were 65 black 5- to 6-month old infants. Caregiving behavior was time sampled and rated on two separate days during two three-hour home visits when the infant was awake. The sampled behaviors included: mutual visual regard, talking to the infant, moving or rocking the infant, contingent vocalization, social play, and caregiver mediation of inanimate objects. At the end of each home visit, ratings were made of the intensity of caregiver expression of positive affect to the infant and of contingency of caregiver response to infant distress. Of the 11 measures of caregiving behavior, five were significantly higher for mothers compared to caregivers (expressing positive affect, social play, variety of social stimulation, social mediation of inanimate objects, and variety of play objects). The other six measures, indexing contingency of response to infant signals and frequencies of visual, vocal, and kinesthetic stimulation, were all higher for mothers, but the differences did not reach statistical significance.

Rubenstein et al. observed that the overall pattern of results indicated that mothers provided a more stimulating and responsive environment than did the caregivers. However, they also found that the amount of time that caregivers had spent with the infants in their care was positively and significantly

related to a number of caregiving behaviors: expression of
positive affect to the infant, talking to the infant, response to
distress, and contingent caregiver vocalization. In short, the
longer a particular child had been with the caregiver, the
greater the likelihood that his or her pattern of interaction
with the infant would approximate that of the mother-infant
interactions.

The Rubenstein et al. study differs from more typical day
care studies in a number of important respects. These infants
were not in group care, but were cared for by a caregiver in
the child's own home. Further, over half (56 percent) of the
caregivers were related to the infants in their care, a circum-
stance which presumably could significantly affect the nature
of the caregiver's relationship to the infant in her care (the
authors do not report whether there were differences between
the related and non-related caregivers in terms of their interactions with the infants). Despite these limitations, this is an
important study insofar as it suggests that given sufficient
exposure, caregivers may increasingly interact with the infants
in their care in ways that are more like mother-infant interactions. From the vantage point of attachment, caregivers are
likely to become an attachment figure for infants precisely to
the degree that their interactions are similar to the interactions
that mothers have with their infants.

Cummings (1980) set out to test the proposition that caregiver stability might be an important variable affecting children's
adjustment to day care. In particular, in one study he examined
differences in children's reactions to being dropped off at the
day care center. On one day the child was left by the mother
with a "stable" caregiver (who had spent an average of 735.8
hours in the center), whereas on the other day the child was
left with a "nonstable" caregiver (average hours at the center
= 323.6). Caregivers were asked to greet the mother and child
from the door of the center as they approached and to take the
child from the mother at the door. For children responding
differently to the stable versus the nonstable caregiver during
transfer, positive affect was more common when observations
involved stable caregivers than when they involved nonstable
caregivers. Further, 13 of the 16 children who differentiated
between caregivers during transfer responded more negatively
during nonstable caregiver transfer than during stable caregiver
transfer.

In a laboratory setting, Cummings found that children
were more likely to seek proximity to the caregiver than to a
stranger, but were less likely to seek proximity to the caregiver

than to the mother. Together, the findings from the laboratory
and the naturalistic observations were taken to indicate that
children formed an "intermediate" attachment to caregivers, a
relationship somewhere between the strong relationship developed
with the mother and the lack of a relationship evident toward
the stranger. Ricciuti (1974) also found that children were
more positive in their response to the approach of caregivers
than to the approach of strangers.

Cummings' emphasis on an "intermediate attachment" is
important, since it underscores the notion that the child's
relationship to the caregiver is substantive and psychologically
important. While perhaps less central than the mother, the
caregiver is not simply a functionary in the child's socioemotional
world. Interestingly, Cohen and Campos (1974) have reported
similar results when comparing children's attachment to their
mothers and fathers. They found that fathers were superior
to strangers as elicitors of attachment behaviors, but that
they were second to mothers.

Finally, Anderson, Nagle, Roberts, and Smith (1981)
examined infants' attachment to their caregivers in the Strange
Situation and found results which bear directly on this question.
As part of their study, they looked at caregiver involvement
as a mediating factor in children's behaviors in the Strange
Situation. Comparing infants' behaviors with their caregivers
and with a stranger, episode by episode, Anderson et al. found
that children displayed significantly more attachment behaviors
toward the caregiver than toward the stranger, thereby supporting Cummings' and Ricciuti's conclusions. However, Anderson
et al. further found that differences in infant Strange Situation
behavior with caregivers were mediated by dimensions of caregiving quality. High caregiver involvement was most consistently
associated with childrens' behaviors indicative of attachment to
the caregiver. On the other hand, low caregiver involvement
was associated with low levels of attachment, affiliative, and
exploratory behaviors in the caregiver's presence. Anderson
et al. observed that children who were with high-involved
caregivers and from centers that were high in physical quality
tended to behave most like the infants described as securely
attached by Ainsworth et al. (1978).

These studies lend empirical support to the theoretical
inferences derived from attachment theory, described earlier
in this chapter. For example, they support Ainsworth's comments
regarding children's attachment to caregivers in the context of
separation from their parents. Specifically, in the context of
"stable" relationships, and in the context of "high-involvement",

children are more likely to display behaviors which have been associated with an attachment relationship.

If, in fact, it is the case that day care infants may become attached to their caregivers in addition to their mothers, it is not clear just how we should understand the relationship and relative status of infants' attachments to each of these adults. In order to evaluate these two relationships further, we specifically compared the Strange Situation behavior of day care infants who experienced the procedure with their mothers on one occasion and with their caregivers on another occasion. These infants generally met the "assumptions" specified above. That is, their day care situation could be construed as meeting the basic conditions for the development of attachment.

METHOD

The families of the infants involved in this study were middle-class, intact, with full-time working mothers, and with infants in full-time day care (Mean = 8.3 hours per day, five days a week). Socioeconomic status was broadly defined by income and education. One criterion was that both parents be high school graduates and that the couple have a combined income between $20,000 and $45,000 per year. Two exceptions included in this study were one mother who did not complete high school but was married to a college graduate and had an administrative position, and one family who made less than $20,000 per year because both parents were in graduate school and working part-time. The mean education level for the mothers in the study was 14.9 years (SD = 2.47). The mean education of the fathers was 15.2 years (SD = 3.98). The mean combined income was $29,000 (SD = $8,710), though only 75 percent of the respondents answered this question.

Virtually all of the mothers (83 percent) reported being pleased with their infants' day care arrangements, the remainder were "ambivalent" about these arrangements, but no mothers reported being greatly dissatisfied with the day care which they had arranged for their infant.

Day Care Center and Subject Selection

Centers were screened using an adaptation of the Menig-Peterson Day Care Questionnaire (1977). In all, ten commercial group centers participated in the study; many of these were church-affiliated. All the centers were considered good quality commercial centers, among the best available, as attested to by long waiting lists of parents desiring to place their children in them. However, none of these centers was a university-affiliated or demonstration type program. Characteristic of these centers was the fact that they had facilities specifically designed or adapted for children, they were safe, clean, with similar caregiver-infant ratios (usually 1:5 or 2:12), and age appropriate toys. All centers met state licensing requirements.

The subjects recruited through these centers were 35 infants (22 male, 13 female), their mothers, and caregivers. All of the infants were between 12 and 18 months of age and had been in full-time day care for at least four months and with the same caregiver for at least three months at the time of their participation in the study. While most of the 15 participating caregivers had little or no formal training in child development (mean education = 12.4 years), then were considered to have a great deal of personal or job-related experience with children, and the five others were considered to have at least some experience. The mean age of the caregivers was 40.3 years (range = 21 to 64 years).

Procedure

Infant attachment to mothers and caregivers was assessed via the Strange Situation, as described in Ainsworth et al. (1978), and conducted in a laboratory observation room at the University of Texas at Austin. The Strange Situation is a series of eight brief episodes during which the infant is observed with his/her mother (the same procedure was used with the caregivers), exposed to a stranger, and separated and reunited with his/her mother. The procedure takes place in a room with two chairs (one for the mother, the other for the stranger) with a pile of toys in the center of the room, equidistant from the two chairs (see Table 4.1).

Two Strange Situation procedures were conducted with each child: one with the child's mother and one with the child's main caregiver from the day care center. These observations were spaced three months apart, with half of the subjects experiencing the procedure with their mothers for the first time, and half experiencing the procedure with their caregivers for the first time. This counterbalancing permitted us to test for possible order effects. Classifications of videotaped observations were made by Sroufe and his colleagues at the University of

Table 4.1 Strange Situation Episodes[a]

Episode[b]	Persons Present
1	Mother (or Caregiver)-Infant-Experimenter
2	Mother-Infant
3	Mother-Infant-Stranger
4	Infant-Stranger
5	Infant-Mother
6	Infant
7	Infant-Stranger
8	Mother-Infant

[a]Adapted from Ainsworth, Blehar, Waters, and Wall (1978).
[b]All episodes after a brief introduction to the room (Episode 1) are 3 minutes in duration unless the child's distress necessitates curtailment or extension of an episode(s).

Minnesota with an interobserver agreement of 92 percent. Coding of specific Strange Situation behaviors was done by a separate group of coders, trained by the researchers, at the University of Texas. In order to establish the reliability of the coders, 25 percent of the subjects were randomly selected to be coded by two different coders. The following behaviors had interrater reliability coefficients equal to or greater than .70: Exploratory Locomotion, Social Locomotion, Total Square Changes, Total Vocalization, Total Smile, Visual Orientation (stranger), Exploratory Visual, Visual Orientation (mother/caregiver), Total Manipulation, Total Crying. Thus, each Strange Situation produced two kinds of data: the attachment classification (which draws most heavily from infant responses to reunion with the mother/caregiver in episodes 5 and 8); and the tabulation of specific behaviors during each episode.

RESULTS

One-way analysis of variance was used in making comparisons between groups on each of the ten variables listed. Preliminary analyses revealed no sex differences and no order effects for attachment behaviors or attachment classifications.

Episode by Episode Comparisons

Table 4.2 shows comparisons (infant-mother versus infant-caregiver) of means for Strange Situation behaviors by episodes. Figures 4.1-4.10 depict these comparisons. Infants showed more exploratory locomotion (Figure 4.1) when they were alone with their mothers than when alone with their caregivers (episodes 2 and 5, $p < .02$ for episode 5). Infants were also considerably more likely to engage in social locomotion (approach the mother/caregiver or the stranger; Figure 4.2) when they were alone with their mothers than when alone with caregivers (episodes 2 and 5, $p < .05$, $p < .07$ respectively), and to attempt to follow the mother as she left the room in episode 6 ($p < .08$). In fact, with the exception of episode 3, where differences were negligible, infants engaged in more social locomotion in every episode in mother-present Strange Situations. Total square changes (Figure 4.3) were also higher when infants were alone with their mothers than when alone with their substitute caregivers (episodes 2 and 5, $p < .07$ and $p < .02$, respectively).

Differences between infant vocalizations to the mother versus the caregiver (Figure 4.4) were not significant, and did not reflect a clear pattern, although infants seemed to vocalize more during episode 2 when with their mothers. Infants smiled (Figure 4.5) more at their mothers in every episode than they did at their caregivers. These differences did not reach statistical significance (there was a weak trend in episode 2 with $p < .11$). Infants also tended to look at the stranger more (Figure 4.6) during Strange Situation procedures with the mother (episodes 3 and 7 $p < .01$ and $p < .06$ respectively); but showed a strong statistical trend ($p < .07$) in episode 8 to look more at the stranger (in those few moments as the stranger exited from the room) when with the caregiver.

Infants consistently displayed higher levels of behavior related to manipulation of objects (Figure 4.7) when with their caregivers in the Strange Situation, although these differences only approached significance in episode 4 ($p < .06$). Infants' crying behavior (Figure 4.8) was quite similar in the presence of both adults, although they were significantly more likely to cry upon the entry of the stranger in episode 3 when with the caregiver ($p < .04$). Differences in exploratory visual (Figure 4.9), and visual orientation toward the mother/caregiver (Figure 4.10) were negligible for both adults.

Table 4.2 Caregiver-Mother Comparisons for Infant Strange Situation Behaviors (Means)

	Episode 2		Episode 3		Episode 4		Episode 5		Episode 6		Episode 7		Episode 8	
	C	M	C	M	C	M	C	M	C	M	C	M	C	M
Exploratory locomotion	4.81	6.13	3.03	2.66	2.53	2.16	3.38	5.06[b]	2.34	2.16	.94	1.16	1.50	1.38
Social locomotion	.81	1.72[a]	1.06	.91	.66	.94	1.53	2.22[a]	.31	.97[a]	.41	.53	1.41	1.56
Total square change	9.47	13.31[a]	5.34	4.31	4.53	3.44	5.16	8.72[b]	3.47	4.00	1.59	1.78	2.41	2.22
Total vocalization	10.81	18.91[a]	7.50	5.50	5.56	7.28	13.44	11.56	4.78	3.09	3.75	3.88	6.84	35.37
Total smile (M/C)	.69	1.41	.34	.49	.11	.19	.66	.73	.0	.30	.03	.0	1.40	2.08
Visual orientation (stranger)	–	–	6.47	8.28[b]	6.38	6.69[a]	2.28	2.06	–	–	7.28	8.72[a]	1.81	1.22
Total manipulation	9.25	9.16	8.44	7.63	8.31	6.38[a]	7.47	7.44	4.44	4.06	4.91	3.69	5.72	5.97
Total crying	.20	.38	.66	.14[b]	3.06	2.65	1.91	2.62	7.31	7.62	3.94	4.00	1.57	2.59
Exploratory visual	15.41	15.66	11.53	12.34	11.56	10.97	12.16	12.72	8.19	7.63	8.56	8.81	11.34	11.25
Visual orientation (M/C)	5.69	5.97	4.78	5.25	4.66	3.38	7.41	7.81	3.72	4.00	2.59	2.78	7.94	8.38[a]

[a] p < .10   [b] p < .05

115

Figure 4.1 Explanatory Locomotion: Episodes—Caregiver vs. Mothers

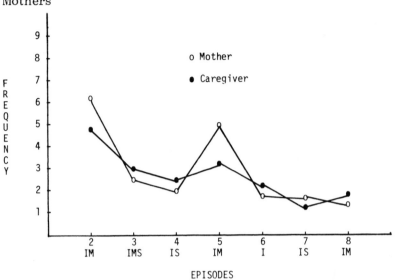

Note: I = Infant; M = Mother; S = Stranger.

Figure 4.2 Social Locomotion—Caregiver/Mother: Episodes—Caregiver vs. Mothers

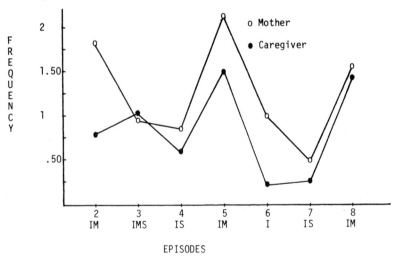

Figure 4.3 Total Square Change: Episodes—Caregiver vs. Mothers

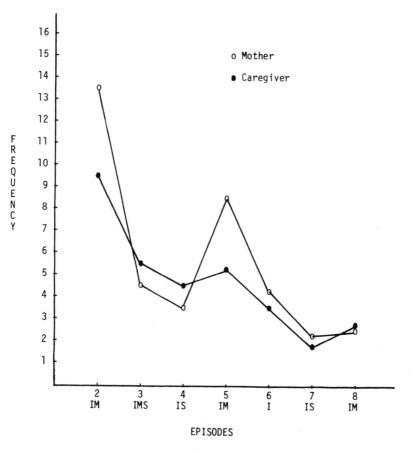

Figure 4.4 Total Vocalization: Episodes−Caregiver vs. Mothers

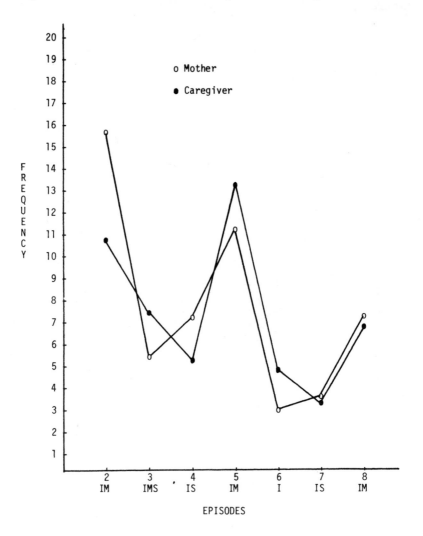

Figure 4.5 Total Smile: Episodes: Caregiver vs. Mothers

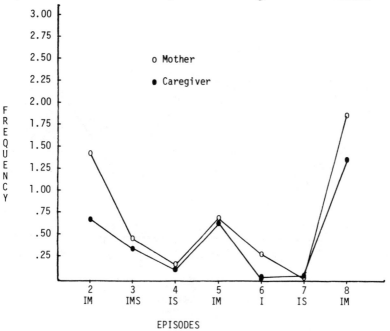

Figure 4.6 Visual Orientation-Stranger: Episodes—Caregiver vs. Mothers

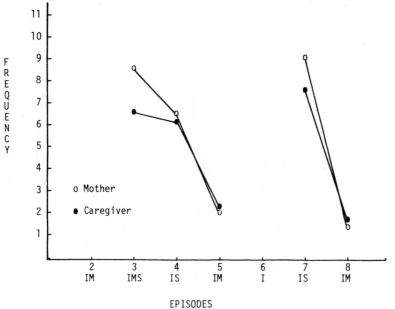

Figure 4.7 Total Manipulation: Episodes−Caregiver vs. Mothers

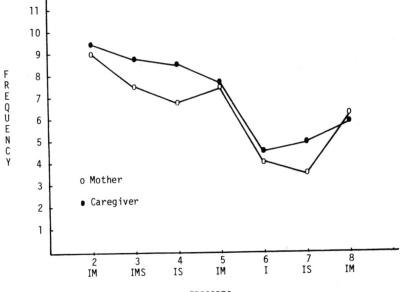

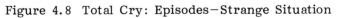

Figure 4.8 Total Cry: Episodes−Strange Situation

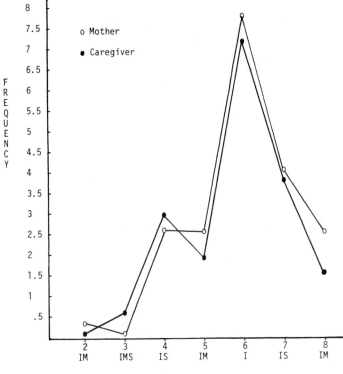

Figure 4.9 Exploratory Visual: Episodes—Caregiver vs. Mothers

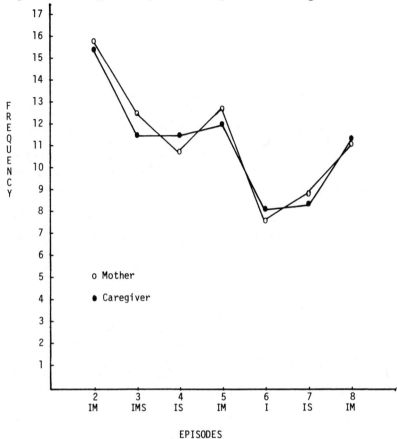

EPISODES

Figure 4.10 Visual Orientation-Mother/Caregiver: Episodes—
Caregiver vs. Mothers

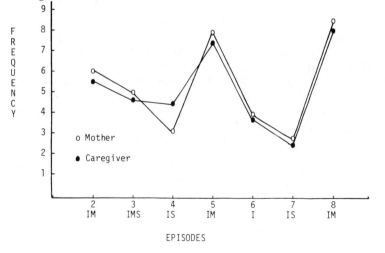

EPISODES

121

Strange Situation Behavior by Attachment
Classification Comparisons

In order to test for differences in attachment behavior as a function of the attachment classifications obtained, comparisons were made between secure (B) and anxiously attached (A and C) infants when they were in the presence of their mothers and caregivers (see Table 4.3). The total incidence of each behavior across episodes was used as the basis for comparison. Six of the ten behaviors tabulated for the Strange Situation showed significant differences between securely and anxiously attached infants when those infants were in the Strange Situation with their mothers. Infants classified as Securely Attached (B) were significantly more likely to smile, vocalize, and explore their environment (exploratory locomotion, total square change, visual exploration) than were infants classified as anxiously attached (avoidant -A- or resistant -C-). On the other hand, the anxiously attached infants cried significantly more than did the securely attached infants. In other words, securely attached infants were able to use mother as a "secure base" and were more sociable. As is evident from Table 4.3, many of these differences were highly significant. However, no significant differences were found for these same behavior-by-classification comparisons when the infants were in the Strange Situation with their caregivers. None of the comparisons even approached statistical significance.

DISCUSSION

Few day care studies have looked at the specific characteristics of the day care child's relationship to his or her caregiver. Instead, research has focused almost exclusively on the possible impact of day care upon the mother-child relationship or on other aspects of development. While this emphasis is readily understandable in terms of the more immediate concerns raised by day care, researchers have more recently begun to explore a broader range of specific questions. Current efforts are increasingly geared toward a more detailed and comprehensive understanding of the day care context, the aim being to optimize the development of children who are placed in substitute care, especially those who spend many hours on a daily basis away from home.

In the present chapter, we have explored the question of children's attachment to their caregivers. A theoretical rationale

Table 4.3 Strange Situation Behaviors (Totals), Caregiver (B vs. A/C) and Mother (B vs. A/C) Comparison

	Caregiver ($A/C_n = 15$, $B_n = 17$)			Mother ($A/C_n = 21$, $B_n = 11$)		
	Mean Value			Mean Value		
	A/C	B	P-value	A/C	B	P-value
Exploratory Locomotion	12.37	20.04	N.S.	13.23	22.89	P < .005
Social Locomotion	7.11	5.10	N.S.	13.23	22.89	N.S.
Total Square Change	31.93	30.92	N.S.	20.79	43.99	P < .005
Total Vocalization (M/C)	56.09	51.31	N.S.	33.48	69.40	P < .03
Total Smile	2.26	3.68	N.S.	2.06	5.43	P < .04
Visual Orientation (stranger)	24.32	25.90	N.S.	28.60	26.03	N.S.
Total Manipulation	43.28	53.21	N.S.	41.63	47.10	N.S.
Total Crying	19.29	14.38	N.S.	32.32	14.25	P < .001
Exploration Visual	7.11	5.10	N.S.	63.63	83.10	P < .001
Visual Orientation (M/C)	37.01	35.84	N.S.	40.05	37.76	N.S.

has been developed to support the thesis that it is necessary
to consider the possibility that children who are in full-time
day care from an early age will become attached to their caregivers. Further, the findings of a number of studies examining
children's relationships to their caregivers have also lent some
support to this view.

Together, the two groups of data from the study reported
herein (Episode by Episode Comparisons, and Strange Situation
Behavior by Classification Comparisons) tend to support the
view garnered from the literature that infants develop an "intermediate" attachment to their caregivers. Clearly, the caregivers
are considerably more than strangers to these infants, otherwise
one would not expect to find attachment behaviors in their
presence. In addition, for a number of behaviors (vocalization,
visual orientation toward the mother/caregiver, visual exploration, crying) differences in infant behavior with each adult were
quite negligible. The lack of significant differences in attachment behaviors with mothers and caregivers could be interpreted
as indicating a degree of similarity in the quality of infants'
relationships with each of these adults, since differences in
Strange Situation attachment behaviors have been related to
differences in caregiver-infant interactions (Anderson et al.
1981) as well as to differences in mother-infant interactions
(Ainsworth, Bell, and Stayton, 1971, 1972). Additionally, the
fact that Sroufe and his colleagues found all but five infant-
caregiver Strange Situations to be classifiable (Ainslie and
Anderson, 1982; Anderson and Ainslie, 1982), also supports
the view that these day care infants had developed important
relationships with their caregivers.

On the other hand, there were a number of notable differences in the infants' behavior with each adult. In particular,
both indices that the child experiences the adult as a "secure
base", and social behaviors showed consistent trends in favor
of the mother-infant Strange Situations (especially in those
episodes where the infant was alone with the mother or caregiver). The strongest trend in the direction of caregiver-infant
Strange Situations was for total manipulation, where infants
consistently engaged in more manipulation of objects when with
their caregivers. Manipulation is clearly the least social of the
behaviors tabulated, since manipulation most often involved
non-social play with toys. Interestingly, this pattern is probably
reflective of differing emphases in each of the child's developmental contexts under consideration (home and day care). In
the day care setting, caregivers are more apt to encourage
children to entertain themselves with toys than to encourage

them to maintain dyadic social exchanges. The clearcut qualitative differences in infant behavior with each of these adults supports the view that infants are more involved with their mothers than with their caregivers, a finding in keeping with other reports in the literature (e.g. Cummings, 1980; Cohen and Campos, 1974; Farran and Ramey, 1977).

To characterize these infants' relationships with their caregivers as reflecting an "intermediate" attachment raises a number of important questions. Previously, we have reported that a comparison of infant-mother and infant-caregiver attachment classifications (derived from the same Strange Situations reported here) suggested that: 1) infants in full-time day care, who had been with the same caregiver for at least three months, did appear to be attached to their caregivers; and 2) that in mother-caregiver comparisons the infants' attachment classifications reflected a slight increase in the number of anxiously attached infants, especially for those classified as anxious-avoidant (A). However, differences in the incidence of secure and anxious attachment classifications for infant-mother versus infant-caregiver were not statistically significant. The distribution of infant-mother attachment classifications (N=34) was as follows: A=9 percent, B=62 percent, C=30 percent. The distribution of infant-caregiver attachment classifications (N=34) was as follows: A=26 percent, B=53 percent, C=21 percent (Ainslie and Anderson, 1982; Anderson and Ainslie, 1982).

The most important issue raised by these data is this: Are these infants really attached to their caregivers? The present comparison of attachment behaviors by attachment classifications raises questions regarding this conclusion. In particular, it is not clear why infant-mother classifications should show such clear differences in terms of infant attachment behaviors during the Strange Situation, while infant-caregiver classifications appear to bear no relationship whatsoever to the attachment behaviors. It is difficult to account for the differences that we have observed on situational grounds. For example, infants who went through the Strange Situation with their mothers were brought to the laboratory by their mothers (usually from home), while caregivers and infants came to the laboratory directly from the center (i.e. mother was not present). In other words, the contextual continuity of the infant's relationship with each adult was maintained. Thus, the data seem to indicate that these infants have developed a relationship with their caregivers. However, it might be best to characterize it as a "familiar" relationship, rather than an attachment relationship. Contrary to our initial impressions, these infants may not, in fact, be attached to their caregivers. This is the view of Sroufe as well (personal communication).

We must also seriously consider the possibility that the Strange Situation procedure is not valid when conducted with caregivers (and perhaps other non-maternal figures, since attempts to validate the procedure have focused almost exclusively on mother-child observations, see Ainsworth et al. 1978). Alternatively, the infant-mother attachment behavior by classification comparisons lends support to the validity of the classifications as a measure of the infant's relationship to the mother, since there were considerable behavioral differences between securely and anxiously attached infants.

These data raise questions regarding how we are to understand qualitative differences in relationships which are important for the young child. As noted earlier, attachment theorists tend to hold two views regarding the nature of that "affectional bond". On the one hand it is viewed as highly specific, and in reference to a particular attachment figure. On the other hand, it is viewed as "predisposing" the child to certain kinds of relationships. The quality of infant attachment behavior when in the Strange Situation with the caregiver might best be described as "diluted". Perhaps in the context of a relatively receptive non-maternal adult, infants are prone to interact in ways that reflect the qualities of the infant's primary attachment relationship (albeit less intensely). In other words, the infant's relationship to primary attachment figures may become generalized to other individuals with whom the child develops substantive (but not attachment) relationships. This may be the reason we see patterns of interaction in the Strange Situation with caregivers which seem classifiable as patterns of attachment, but which seem to lack vitality when we compare mother and caregiver classifications and behaviors.

While this view is appealing, it is not without problems. For example, it does not account for the fact that children have been found to have different attachment relationships to their mothers and fathers (e.g. Main and Weston, 1981). An overemphasis on generalization fails to take into account the possibility of genuine multiple attachments. It also implies a view of infant-adult relationships as unidirectional, a view which is highly questionable. In short, these findings raise questions regarding the nature of multiple attachments and how we should understand qualitative differences in these. A corollary problem is whether it is possible to distinguish "true" attachment relationships from relationships in which the infant may be quite familiar with an adult, but not necessarily attached to that adult. The results of the present study suggest that attachment classification by Strange Situation behavior comparisons may be necessary to distinguish between relationships characterized by a high "familiarity" and attachment relationships.

Ainsworth (1972) has voiced strong reservations regarding the notion of intensity or strength of attachment, preferring instead to focus on the quality of attachment. For example, Ainsworth notes that "It is by no means evident that strength of attachment is an especially useful dimension . . . if an infant has insufficient interaction with any one figure, he may not become attached to anyone. There is, to date, no empirical evidence which suggests that differing strengths of attachment are associated with different qualitative outcomes, or which enables us to identify conditions associated with differing strengths of attachment. On the other hand, both clinical and recent research findings strongly suggest that qualitative differences in infant-mother attachment relations are associated both with qualitative differences in antecedent maternal behaviors and with different behavioral outcomes in the case of the child. Therefore, although it seems fruitless in the present state of knowledge to attempt to assess strength of attachment, it seems useful to evaluate the quality of the attachment relationship" (p. 120). Thus, attachment theorists would also most likely view the present infant-caregiver results as reflecting a relationship of familiarity, rather than reflecting an "intermediate" attachment.

The actual status of infant-caregiver relationships may be difficult to determine. This is the case in part because the construct of attachment may not adequately differentiate between different types of relationships which may be of moment for the young child, but which may not necessarily be attachment relationships in the sense in which these theorists use the term. Ainsworth herself (1972) has commented that the distinction between attachment figure and playmate, or attachment versus affiliative tendencies (and, we might add, attachment versus familiarity) require further efforts at clarification. Such clarification is precisely what is needed in order to adequately understand the day care child's relationship to his or her caregiver.

Finally, we return to the question of whether or not it is desirable for infants to become attached to their caregivers in the context of full-time day care. What are the consequences of the alternatives? Attachment theorists have accumulated considerable support for their view that secure attachment is very important for a child's socioemotional development. Given

that a large percentage of young children are now in substitute
care, the advantages and disadvantages of their developing a
close relationship to their caregiver must be considered. It
seems evident that, in a developmental context in which the
child spends many hours away from home every day, it is in
the best interest of the child to be in the care of an adult with
whom he or she feels safe, cared for, and responded to. Looked
at from this perspective, optimal infant-caregiver relationships
would be those which are closest to being attachment relationships, since there is some evidence to suggest that these would
reflect interactions which are responsive and sensitive. In the
present study, it seems probable that infants who were originally
classified as securely attached (53 percent) were infants who
had better relationships with their caregivers (irrespective of
whether or not they were "actually" attached), while those
with anxious attachments (47 percent) had relationships that
were less adequate. The latter group may warrant concern,
especially in those cases where infants were classified as
anxiously-attached with both their mothers and their caregivers
(29 percent of the cases).

It may be that the relief engendered by early research
regarding day care children's preference for their mother over
the caregiver requires some reconsideration. It is readily
understandable that parents would want their children to prefer
them over the children's caregivers. However, as Ainsworth
(1972) has noted, such a preferential relationship is not necessarily threatened by other close relationships. Thus, parents,
day care staff, and researchers need to direct their efforts
toward maximizing the quality of the relationship that the child
is able to develop with a caregiver, a relationship which is
most likely to be conducive to optimal socioemotional development. From this vantage point, it may be that infant-caregiver
attachment is something to be desired, rather than feared.

REFERENCES

Ainslie, R. C. The Psychology of Twinship. Lincoln: University
    of Nebraska Press, in press.

Ainslie, R. C., and Anderson, C. W. Maternal perceptions of
    their infants' day care. Infant Mental Health Journal, in
    press.

Ainslie, R. C., and Anderson, C. W. Caregiver-infant inter-
    action in the day care setting and infants' characteristics.
    Paper presented at the meeting of the American Psychological
    Association, Washington, D.C., 1982.

Ainsworth, M. D. S. Infancy in Uganda: Infant care and the
    growth of love. Baltimore: Johns Hopkins University Press,
    1967.

Ainsworth, M. D. S. Object relations, dependency, and attach-
    ment: A theoretical review of the infant-mother relationship.
    Child Development, 1969, 40, 969-1025.

Ainsworth, M. D. S. Attachment and dependency: A comparison.
    In J. L. Gewirtz (Ed.), Attachment and Dependency.
    Washington, D.C.: V. H. Winston, 1972.

Ainsworth, M. D. S. The development of infant-mother attach-
    ment. In B. M. Caldwell and H. N. Ricciuti (Eds.), Review
    of child development research (Vol. 3). Chicago: University
    of Chicago Press, 1973.

Ainsworth, M. D. S., and Bell, S. M. Attachment, exploration,
    and separation: Illustrated by the behavior of one year-olds
    in a strange situation. Child Development, 1970, 41, 49-67.

Ainsworth, M. D. S., Bell, S. M., and Stayton, D. J. Individ-
    ual differences in strange situation behavior of one year-olds.
    In H. R. Schaffer (Ed.), The origins of human social relations.
    London and New York: Academic Press, 1971.

Ainsworth, M. D. S., Bell, S. M., and Stayton, D. J. Individ-
    ual differences in the development of some attachment
    behaviors. Merrill-Palmer Quarterly 1972, 18, 123-143.

Ainsworth, M. D. S., Blehar, M. C., Waters, E., and Wall, S.
    Patterns of attachment: A psychological study of the strange
    situation. New York: John Wiley & Sons, 1978.

Anderson, C. W., and Ainslie, R. C. Quality of day care as
    a mediator of mother-infant attachment. Paper presented
    at the meetings of the Southwestern Psychological Association,
    Dallas, Texas, 1982.

Anderson, C. W., Nagle, R. J., Roberts, W. A., and Smith, J. W. Attachment to substitute caregivers as a function of center quality and caregiver involvement. Child Development 1981, 52, 53-61.

Arend, R., Gove, F. L., and Sroufe, L. A. Continuity of individual adaptation from infancy to kindergarten: A predictive study of ego-resiliency and curiosity in preschoolers. Child Development, 1979, 50, 950-959.

Belsky, J., and Steinberg, L. The effects of day care: A critical review. Child Development, 1978, 49, 929-949.

Bronfenbrenner, U. The ecology of human development. Cambridge, Massachusetts: Harvard University Press, 1979.

Cairns, R. Attachment and dependency: A psychobiological and social-learning synthesis. In J. L. Gewirtz (Ed.), Attachment and dependency. Washington, D.C.: V. H. Winston, 1972.

Cohen, L. J., and Campos, J. J. Father, mother, and stranger as elicitors of attachment behavior in infancy. Developmental Psychology, 1974, 10, 146-154.

Cummings, E. M. Caregiver stability and day care. Developmental Psychology, 1980, 16, 31-37.

Farran, D., and Ramey, C. Infant day care and attachment behaviors toward mothers and teachers. Child Development, 1977, 48, 1112-1116.

Gewirtz, J. L. Attachment, dependence, and a distinction in terms of stimulus control. In J. L. Gewirtz (Ed.), Attachment and dependency. Washington, D.C., V. H. Winston, 1972a.

Grossmann, K., and Grossmann, K. E. Maternal sensitivity to infants' signals during the first year as related to the year old's behavior in Ainsworth's Strange Situation in a sample of Northern German families. Paper presented to the International Conference on Infant Studies, Austin, Texas, 1982.

Kagan, J., Kearsley, R., and Zelazo, P. Infancy: Its place
in human development. Cambridge, Massachusetts: Harvard
University Press, 1978.

Lamb, M. E., Thompson, R. A., Gardner, W., Charnoy, E. L.,
and Estes, D. Security of infantile attachment as assessed
in the "Strange Situation": Its study and biological interpretation. In Behavioral and brain sciences, 1983.

Main, M., and Weston, D. Security of attachment to mother
and father: Related to conflict behavior and readiness to
establish new relationships. Child Development, 1981, 52,
932-940.

Matas, L., Arend, R. A., and Sroufe, L. A. Continuity of
adaptation in the second year: The relationship between
quality of attachment and later competence. Child Development, 1978, 49, 547-556.

Ricciuti, H. Fear and development of social attachments in the
first year of life. In M. Lewis and L. A. Rosenblum (Eds.),
The Origins of Human Behavior: Fear. New York: John
Wiley & Sons, 1974.

Robertson, J., and Robertson, J. Young children in brief
separation. Film No. 1: Kate, aged 2 years 5 months, in
foster-care for 27 days. London: Tavistock Institute of
Human Relations, 1968.(a) (New York: New York University
Film Library.)

Robertson, J., and Robertson, J. Young children in brief
separation. Film No. 2: Jane, 17 months, in foster-care
for 10 days. London: Tavistock Institute of Human Relations,
1968.(b) (New York: New York University Film Library.)

Rubenstein, J., Pedersen, R., and Yarrow, L. What happens
when mother is away: a comparison of mothers and substitute
caregivers. Developmental Psychology, 1977, 13, 529-530.

Rutter, M. Social-emotional consequences of day care for preschool children. American Journal of Orthopsychiatry, 1981,
51, 4-28.

Schaffer, H. R., and Emerson, P. E. The development of social
attachments in infancy. Monographs of the Society for Research in Child Development, 1964 (a), 29 (3, Serial No. 94).

Sroufe, L. A. The coherence of individual development.
  American Psychologist, 1979, 34, 834-841.

Sroufe, L. A., and Waters, E. Attachment as an organizational
  construct. Child Development, 1977, 48, 1184-1199.

Sroufe, L. A., and Fleeson, J. Attachment and the construction
  of relationships. In Z. Rubin and W. W. Hartup (Eds.),
  Relationships: Their role in children's development. New
  York: Cambridge University Press, in press.

Weinraub, M., Brooks, J., and Lewis, M. The social network:
  A reconsideration of the concept of attachment. Human
  Development, 1977, 20, 31-47.

5.

Allegiances or Attachments: Relationships among Infants and Their Day Care Teachers

Dale C. Farran, Margaret Burchinal, Susan East Hutaff, and Craig T. Ramey

The growth in social responsiveness of infants to people in their environment has been hypothesized by Shaffer and Emerson (1964) as a developmental progression occurring in three stages. The last stage, attachment to specific individuals, appears between six and nine months of age, and becomes more intense around twelve months. In group day care, infants are exposed to a social environment composed of more types and numbers of people available for interaction than traditionally found in the home. Although Fein and Clark-Stewart (1973) have stated that it is reasonable to expect that specific social discriminations would be more difficult in a large group environment such as day care, as of yet, those discriminations remain relatively uncharted.

Infants who are placed into group day care spend a substantial portion of their day in what may be termed a polymatric situation. They encounter a number of adult caregivers who all function to some degree in the maternal role. Even in day care situations where teachers are assigned to specific children, it has been shown that more than 50 percent of the child's interactions are with adults other than the assigned one (Wilcox, Staff and Romaine, undated). Various researchers (Ainsworth, 1973; Rutter, 1981) and others interested in public policy (Fowler, 1975) have been concerned about the effect such an environment may have on the child's social development, particularly if day care is begun in early infancy during the months when an attachment bond is formed to a primary caregiver. Several studies have compared the attachment relationship between mothers and infants to that between the infants and their alternative caregivers (Farran and Ramey, 1977; Kagan, Kearsley, and Zelazo, 1976; Krentz, 1983). Few have examined the social environment of the day care nursery to determine the number and quality of interactions occurring there and their possible significance for attachment relationships within the context of day care. This facet of this issue is concerned with how the infant differentiates among the alternative care- givers that the day care situation provides. Is the infant forming a preferential relationship with a single day care teacher? Does that relationship, if it exists, serve as an attach- ment bond? If preferences emerge, when do they? Is it at the same time as attachment seems to develop to the mother were the child at home? These are intriguing questions which have implications both for our understanding of the process of social development in infancy and for our understanding of the effects of a major alternative in rearing environments for children, as we move more and more toward a society of working mothers whose infants are in care.

METHOD

Subjects

The group consisted of 15 infants, who were placed in day care between the ages of six weeks and three months, and their teachers. The children constituted the entire nursery group in an early intervention project at the Frank Porter Graham Child Development Center. The 15 nursery infants had been randomly assigned to receive day care out of the entire "cohort" of 30 infants who had been selected for partici- pation in the project because they were considered at "high risk" for later intellectual retardation by virtue of such socio- economic characteristics of their families as low maternal IQ, poverty, and low levels of paternal and maternal education. Fourteen of the infants were black; 10 of the 15 were male.

The data from one black, male child were excluded from analysis because he exhibited severe organically-based develop- mental delays. The child was removed from the nursery between nine and twelve months of age so that more appropriate help could be provided for him.

The infants spent about seven hours per day, five days a week at the Center in a contiguous set of four rooms and a long hallway with five primary teachers. Two of the teachers were male; four were black. All teachers had received early

childhood teacher training either through formal schooling or
in-service training. They had a minimum of 18 months of
prior teaching experience. Teachers were not assigned to
particular children; specific curriculum assignments were
rotated among the teachers so that all teachers interacted with
all the children. The nursery consisted of two primary play
rooms, a long hallway which served as a feeding area and
additional play room, and two sleeping rooms. Children and
teachers moved freely among the two play rooms and the hallway.
Substitute teachers, medical staff members, and other center
employees also occasionally interacted with the infants in the
nursery.

The infants did not all enter the center in a group; the
age spread between the oldest and the youngest was eight
months. The number of children in the nursery increased from
four to fifteen over a span of seven months as the children
reached the minimum entrance age of six weeks. The number
of teachers also increased as the number of the children in the
nursery increased. Initially, there were three black teachers,
two females and one male. As infant enrollment increased, a
white male, and a black female teacher were added permanently
to the teaching staff.

Instruments

A coding scheme was developed to describe the interactions
between the nursery children and their teachers. Interactions
among the children were also of interest. The specific behaviors
observed were those which had previously been termed attachment behaviors: looking, vocalizing, touching, holding, mutual
play, active proximity seeking, and general proximity of children
and teachers to each other. Particular interest was paid to the
individuals with whom the child was interacting; toward whom
the child made social overtures; and who made social overtures
toward the child.

Each observation spanned 25 minutes. The behaviors of
the infant being observed and the behaviors of others toward
the infant were recorded in ten-second blocks. Four minutes
of data were collected followed by a one minute pause. During
this pause, information regarding context was recorded. Three
categories of behaviors were coded: (1) the target child's behaviors, the child's social overtures toward others and the
child's motoric behaviors; (2) the social or caretaking behaviors
of others toward the target child; and (3) the general social

categories of proximity and mutual play. The categories and
their conventions are listed in Table 5.1. Any observed social
behavior that was either directed toward the target child or
directed toward another by the target child was coded by
indicating who the other person involved in the overture or
interaction was, while recording the type of specific behavior
observed. Thus, the number and types of overtures or interactions made by each infant toward each teacher could be tallied
as well as the number and types of socially directed behavior
that each teacher exhibited toward each infant. In addition,
the number of instances of nondirected vocalizations, crawling,
walking, and playing alone with toys were scored as well as to
whom, if anyone, the child was in proximity.

Data collection began after about three weeks of training
when the three female experimenters reached the criterion of
80 percent total agreement across all categories. The reliability
of each category was scored by dividing the number of behaviors
within that category observed by both experimenters (agreements) by the total number of behaviors observed by either
experimenter (agreements plus disagreements). The total
reliability for that observation was computed by summing the
agreements across categories, summing the agreements plus
disagreements across categories, and dividing the agreements
by the agreements plus disagreements.

Reliability among experimenters was checked on 14 sessions
during data collection. Percent agreement for child behaviors
averaged 82 percent across behaviors for occurrence and 74
percent across behaviors for direction. For teacher behaviors
percent agreement averaged 69 percent across categories for
occurrence and 66 percent for direction.

Procedure

The infants were observed for eight 25-minute sessions
spread over a three week period at each of three ages: six,
nine, and twelve months. Data were recorded continuously in
ten-second blocks on the interactions between the target child
and the teachers or peers, noting both the behaviors of the
child toward particular teachers or peers and the teachers or
peers who were directing behaviors toward the child. There
were six infants receiving day care and three permanent teachers
when the six-month data were collected on the oldest children.
By the time that the oldest children were nine months old, all
15 infants were receiving day care within the nursery. All 15

Table 5.1 Categories for Nursery Observation of Social Interactions

---

GENERAL CATEGORIES

Proximity
Child is within three feet of anyone in the room. Coded by letters indicating who is in proximity. Initiation by the target child is indicated by a subscript of R (e.g., J_R) and initiation of proximity by anyone else is coded by a subscript of I (e.g., J_I).

Mutual Play
Infant and teacher are both involved with a toy either through mutual contact with toy or convention. Mutual play may be without toys as well: 1) Teacher and child are engaged in rhythmical, predictable set of behaviors as in a game, e.g., pat-a-cake. 2) Teacher and infant are engaged in affectionate interaction, repetitive nuzzling, repetitive verbalizations. For mutual play to be scored without toys, behavior must be somewhat ritualized, not brief affection, and both partners must be actively attentive to each other. Scored by letter indicating who is playing with the target child.

Mutual plays
a) When a teacher is demonstrating a toy and has infant's prolonged attention or active attempt to contact toy by infant, code it MP and EG for the teacher.
b) When the teacher and child are mutually playing with toy, score M and MP.
c) When the teacher and child are engaged in rhythmical game, for example pat-a-cake, score it as MP.

CHILD CATEGORIES

Vocalization
A v is any verbal utterance by the target child other than crying or grunts. A check indicates a nondirectional vocalization and a letter indicates who the vocalization is directed toward, this is determined by the child's gaze at a particular person's face or following a vocalization by another specifically directed to the child.

(continued)

137

Table 5.1 (continued)

Look
A look occurs when the child's eyes are fixated on the upper part of a person's body (coded by letter). He may look at more than one person during the ten-second block (each coded by letter).

To score an L when child is looking at the toy a teacher is demonstrating, the teacher must be within the child's peripheral vision.

Cry
Child is crying. This is scored by level: 1) fussing-noncontinuous cry, 2) crying-continuous whining, 3) loud crying-continuous wail, screaming, red-raced.

Must start out with a 1) level cry, unless start of session or sheet when child is crying.

Reach
This occurs when a child's arm(s) are extended toward a particular person (coded by letter). Reach not scored toward toys.

Touch
This is when the child's hand(s) touch any part of a person or their clothing (on them). It is coded by letter. Code touch when child is holding onto teacher to stand up. Includes kissing by child.

Crawling
Child is locomoting self, can be crawling or bellycrawling (using arms). To be scored there must be distance covered. If crawling toward someone, code by letter, person to whom crawling is directed.

If child is walking code W under crawl (CR)

Table 5.1 (continued)

Manipulate
   Child is tactily exploring toy* in any fashion. It must be
   active, not just gross motor activity. Includes active jumping
   in jumper seat.

   *toy = any separate object from the child which the child is
   exploring—door jambs, edge of walker. Does not include
   holding on to side of object (walker or crib) in order to pull
   up or keep from falling.

Extend/Give
   Child has toy in hand and extends and/or gives it to a teacher
   coded by letter of that person. Child is pointing at teacher
   or actively holding out their hands to teacher.

TEACHER CATEGORIES

Vocalization
   This is any verbal utterance directed at the target child.
   Coded by letter of vocalizer. If the teacher is not in proximity
   to child (three feet), she must mention child by name, be
   looking at child, or be vocalizing in clear response to behavior
   of child.

Look
   This occurs when the teacher's eyes are fixated on the target
   child. Coded by letter of looker.

Touch
   Teacher's hand touches any part of target child or teacher's
   arm is around child. It must be purposeful touch (child can
   be touching teacher, leaning against her, without teacher
   touching child in purposeful way).

   Whenever teacher touches child, even in going to HOLD,
   score T-touch.

(continued)

Table 5.1 (continued)

Score touch when teacher is supporting child—but his feet are still on ground (e.g., walking).

During caregiving, touch is scored only if the teacher is touching child to engage their attention (e.g., tickling).

Hold
Hold occurs when teacher is supporting the child's weight; child must be off the ground. Teacher is stationary.

Carry
Teacher is supporting all of the child's weight. Teacher is transporting child from place to place.

Extend/Give
Teacher has toy in hand and extends, demonstrates, and/or gives it to child. Teacher may also be demonstrating or attempting to interest child in toys over several ten-second blocks—if child responds, then score MP also.

To code EG, the teacher must be trying to get the child to do something, for example, only code teacher clapping as EG when teacher is showing child something to do.

When child is in jumper seats code EG if teacher bounces child.

Caregiving
This is an action by teacher that is related to the physical well-being of the child, e.g. wiping nose, changing diapers, etc.

Does not include diaper checking.

---

infants were in the nursery when the six-month data were
collected on the youngest six infants.

Observations were collected only if there were at least
five awake children in the nursery and at least three teachers
present. An infant was not selected to be observed if (s)he
was being fed, having diapers changed, asleep, or engaged in
a curriculum activity with a teacher. However, if the target
child did engage in any of these activities during an observation,
then the remainder of that four minutes of continuous data
collection was completed by marking that the activity was occuring
as well as recording the other behaviors that occurred. The
observation was then discontinued and data collection was
resumed only if the activity lasted less than 30 minutes. If
the observation was continued, then the length of time of the
interruption was noted.

RESULTS

In summarizing the observational data at three ages for
each of the infants, two issues were of interest. The first
issue involves describing the social environment of infants in
group day care, focusing on the characteristics of the interactions among the adults and the children. The second issue
involves the possibility that attachment relationships were
developing between particular teachers and children. This
latter issue is of interest because the period from six to twelve
months is the time when one witnesses the growth of attachment
behaviors of infants with their parents. Given that a day care
environment is quite different from what most infants experience,
the question is, are similar attachments developing with the
individuals who are part of the group day care environment?

The Social Environment of Group Day Care

On the face of it, infant day care appears to be quite
different from the environment most infants experience. Even
those infants who are developing in large families experience a
fewer number of adults interacting with them during the day
and peers who are multiaged rather than all within eight months
of each other. Group day care environments are busy places.
University-based, research-oriented day care centers may be
even busier. In our case, in addition to the five regular
teachers and 14 infants, there were numerous visitors to the

day care center. Teachers of older children sometimes took
their breaks and came in to play with the infants; graduate
students were often around; the medical staff regularly employed
nurses and assistants to administer medicine, take temperatures
and remove children for examinations. Almost all of this activity
took place within two rooms and a long hallway. Thus, children
were constantly stimulated and to some degree involved, being
removed only for periods of sleep.

    The questions we have asked about that environment are:

1. How did the children's behaviors change across time?
2. How were their social behaviors distributed among the
   possible recipients for social interactions in the daycare?
3. Did those recipients and initiators of social interaction
   change across the ages studied?
4. What is the relationship between the social behaviors
   directed toward the child and the child's social behaviors
   directed towards others?

    The primary means for the analysis of these data was a
series of repeated measures multivariate analyses of variance
(MANOVA) using the McCall and Appelbaum (1977) transforma-
tions. Social interactive overtures by infants were collapsed
across teachers; overtures by teachers toward the infants were
also collapsed across teachers. We then compared behaviors
directed toward and received from teachers to those directed
toward and received from peers and from other adults at each
age. Another set of MANOVAs assessed the change in infant,
teacher, and peer behaviors across time.

General Description of Changes in Behavior Across Time

    While they were awake, infants spent about 50 percent or
more of their time interacting with toys alone as shown in Table
5.2. Interacting with toys means that a toy was within three
feet of the child and he or she was engaged with it in some way.
There was no significant change in the amount of time the infants
spent manipulating toys alone across the ages studied. Certainly
there were qualitative changes in what the infants did with the
toys, but the amount of time they spent with toys alone was
relatively the same at each of the three ages.

    Two other behaviors did show significant changes across
time. Children changed significantly in the amount of time
they spent moving around the environment, obviously connected
to the motoric changes which are occuring at these same ages.
At six months, infants moved around the nursery about 11 per-

Table 5.2 Social Behaviors Directed by the Infants to Others at Six, Nine, and Twelve Months

	Six Months M SD (Range)	Nine Months M SD (Range)	Twelve Month M SD (Range)
Vocalizations			
Teachers	15.2 12.0 (1-37)	23.6 17.6 (1-63)	38.0 26.9 (6-99)
Peers	7.1 8.8 (0-31)	14.6 11.6 (2-44)	16.2 14.3 (2-57)
Non-directed	131.6 80.7 (7-272)	141.4 60.8 (59-255)	103.4 64.5 (17-227)
Crying	53.4 33.9 (15-151)	50.4 37.8 (3-134)	31.8 20.6 (3-75)
Extending/Giving Toys			
Teachers	0.1 0.3 (0-1)	1.6 2.8 (0-10)	12.0 10.1 (1-31)
Peers	0.1 0.3 (0-1)	1.4 2.2 (0-8)	2.4 2.6 (0-7)
Play			
Teachers	35.1 29.3 (3-118)	33.8 26.1 (7-113)	74.7 57.4 (15-231)
Peers	9.2 10.1 (0-37)	32.4 20.6 (0-74)	41.1 33.9 (7-123)
Alone	527.9 114.5 (258-714)	529.5 88.5 (384-705)	542.8 77.5 (395-689)
Touch			
Teachers	47.1 51.3 (0-188)	65.0 35.1 (10-129)	52.8 25.8 (13-99)
Peers	17.3 11.4 (1-45)	15.6 8.9 (4-34)	18.8 10.2 (4-44)

(continued)

Table 5.2 (continued)

	Six Months M SD (Range)	Nine Months M SD (Range)	Twelve Months M SD (Range)
Locomotion			
Teachers	14.5 12.6 (5-70)	29.5 19.8 (5-70)	26.0 12.4 (10-50)
Peers	13.4 12.8 (0-49)	11.9 8.3 (1-30)	5.7 3.4 (0-12)
Non-directed	110.6 71.8 (6-221)	215.5 89.3 (98-428)	233.8 66.7 (144-383)
Proximity			
Teachers	402.1 92.5 (271-585)	379.5 107.9 (224-593)	492.2 98.8 (358-716)
Peers	545.0 86.9 (402-681)	526.7 77.3 (392-653)	607.6 80.7 (465-732)
Alone	262.3 82.8 (6-221)	272.7 53.7 (161-376)	180.8 72.7 (54-328)
Look			
Teachers	253.6 60.4 (154-362)	286.7 65.9 (202-392)	296.1 53.6 (222-391)
Peers	227.4 69.3 (163-394)	251.9 58.6 (154-361)	278.6 79.0 (177-430)

Note Data are the number of ten-second blocks out of a total of 960 ten-second blocks.

cent of the time; many of the infants were crawling at least marginally by six months. There was a significant increase in the amount of time spent moving around the nursery between six and nine months; in fact the percentage doubled between those two ages. There was no further change between nine and twelve months. Interestingly, there was also a change from six to twelve months in how much time infants were alone in the environment; alone being defined as having no other person within a three-foot radius—or arm's reach. At six and nine months, infants were alone a little more than one-quarter of time. That percentage decreased to 19 percent at twelve months, a significant change. It is possible that once the infants could walk or crawl with dexterity, they were able to control their environment to a greater degree and could bring themselves into contact with other people.

Finally, both vocalizations and crying changed significantly over time. Non-directed vocalizations were those sounds made by the infants which were not addressed to anyone in particular. Often these sounds were made as an accompaniment to the infant's play. These non-fussy sounds which were not particularly directed to anyone were in evidence about 14 percent of the time at both six and nine months and showed a significant decline between nine and twelve months. As we shall see later, there was a significant increase in the amount of directed vocalizations between nine and twelve months. Crying decreased significantly over time, showing the greatest change between nine and twelve months.

Directed Social Behaviors: A Comparison of Targets

It is apparent from Table 5.2 that despite the number and variety of people available in the day care nursery, the five teachers were by far the most salient people there as far as the infants' social behaviors were concerned. At each age, the infants vocalized more to the teachers than to peers, touched teachers more than peers, moved toward teachers more than toward peers, and engaged in more mutual play with teachers. We compared the amount of social initiations directed toward teachers compared to other adults who were present in the nursery, comparing the five teachers against the total of all social initiations directed toward all other adults. Although those figures are not presented in Table 5.2, the analyses demonstrated that few social bids were directed toward other adults. The salient feature of the teachers present in the nursery was apparently not their number but their status in the eyes of the infants.

Behaviors which could be considered more passive did not differentiate among targets for social interactions in the nursery. Children actually spent more time in proximity to peers overall than they did to teachers. There were no differences at any age in the amount of looking infants did at teachers when compared to peers.

Teachers may have been the most prominent individuals for the infants because they were the most active in their behaviors toward the infants. Table 5.3 compares the social bids of teachers and peers directed toward the target children at each of the ages. (We also compared the behaviors of the five teachers to the sum total of the behaviors of all other adults in the environment. Visiting adults, substitutes, graduate students, and the like were relatively inactive participants in the nursery and did not seem to constitute much of a presence there.) At each age and for each behavior teachers were significantly more active than peers toward the target children.

Social Behaviors Compared Across the Ages

The social behavior of infants directed toward others in the nursery and of others' behaviors directed toward the infants at all three ages are summarized in Tables 5.2 and 5.3. Teacher behaviors toward the infants were not very different at the three ages assessed. There were no significant differences among the ages in how much teachers touched, held, or looked at the infants. They did change in two other major categories, and both of those changes seemed to occur primarily between the ages of nine and twelve months. At twelve months teachers vocalized significantly more to the target child than they did to that child at nine months. They also extended or gave toys significantly more at twelve months. These were meaningful changes in the two behaviors. The number of times a teacher extended a toy to an infant doubled between those two ages. Extending a toy served often as the beginning of a mutual play episode; there were sometimes several observational blocks where a teacher would demonstrate the way a toy worked in an attempt to engage the child in play. Teachers may have viewed the children as more competent and therefore as more able to respond to extended initiations and demonstrations of toys.

Peer behavior directed toward the target infant was also relatively constant at the three ages. The only change in the kinds of bids directed by peers toward the infant occurred in vocalizations which increased significantly between six and nine months and again between nine and twelve months.

Table 5.3 Social Behaviors of Teachers and Peers Directed to the Infants at Six, Nine, and Twelve Months

	Six Months		Nine Months		Twelve Months	
	M	SD	M	SD	M	SD
	(Range)		(Range)		(Range)	
Vocalizations						
Teachers	127.4	47.4	126.7	52.5	185.1	55.6
	(62-223)		(41-218)		(100-299)	
Peers	5.8	5.0	9.8	8.9	14.1	8.4
	(0-15)		(0-31)		(5-34)	
Extending/Giving Toy						
Teachers	48.3	29.6	40.0	23.7	87.6	52.2
	(10-120)		(4-106)		(33-231)	
Peers	0.6	1.2	0.6	1.2	0.9	1.6
	(0-4)		(0-4)		(0-6)	
Touch						
Teachers	47.1	51.3	61.0	30.9	70.6	25.9
	(0-188)		(7-119)		(22-131)	
Peers	14.5	9.5	13.6	9.6	12.8	7.9
	(4-35)		(6-36)		(1-27)	
Look						
Teachers	287.9	73.1	252.2	74.6	306.7	61.7
	(168-385)		(89-336)		(61-207)	
Peers	75.8	38.7	95.9	34.3	88.5	24.5
	(16-136)		(54-156)		(48-135)	
Hold						
Teachers	56.2	45.0	55.3	36.1	56.0	45.2
	(2-151)		(6-125)		(6-185)	

147

Infant behavior, especially as it was manifested in social bids toward the teachers, changed a great deal across the three ages, primarily between nine and twelve months. In general, infants were significantly more in proximity to teachers at twelve months than they had been at nine months. There was also a significant change in the amount of time infants were engaged in play with the teachers; this activity more than doubled between nine and twelve months. On the other hand, playful interactions with peers almost doubled between six and nine months but showed no significant change between nine and twelve months. It should be noted that not much of the infant's time was spent playing with teachers or with peers. Play with teachers occurred somewhat under ten percent of the time at the most active age, twelve months.

Children appeared to be developing more sophisticated skills for initiating interactions with the adults in the room across the ages. Most notable was the increase in their ability to extend toys to the adults. These bids usually involved an initiation by the child toward beginning a mutual play episode. They constituted episodes when the child would bring a toy to an adult. Selecting an object and then bringing it to the adult's attention is a very complex behavior which was not seen at all at six months, rarely at nine months and somewhat more frequently at twelve months.

The infants' vocalizations at six, nine, and twelve months illustrate the process of the growth of differential social responsiveness occurring in the nursery. Figure 5.1 shows the amount of vocalization by infants at each of the three ages broken down into two main types—directed and non-directed. Within the directed bar, vocalizations are again divided; the solid section indicates vocalizations directed to teachers; the cross-hatched, vocalizations directed to peers. As you can see, from six to nine months there was relatively little change in vocalizations either directed or non-directed. At six and nine months approximately 80 percent of vocalizations were non-directed with the remaining 20 percent about evenly divided between teachers and peers. At twelve months, 65 percent of vocalizations were non-directed and 25 percent were directed to teachers. From nine to twelve months, the amount of vocalizations which were non-directed significantly decreased and the amount directed to teachers significantly increased.

Individual Differences

In describing the changes that occurred with the group of infants across the ages, we have not shown the extent of individ-

Figure 5.1 Change in the Proportion of Vocalizations Which
Were Directed to Others at Six, Nine, and Twelve Months

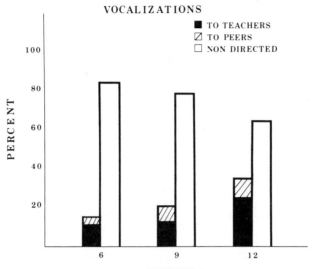

MONTHS

ual differences among the infants in terms of behaviors directed
toward them by teachers. One can get some notion of the extent
of these differences by looking at the ranges presented for
each behavior in parentheses in Table 5.2. For example the
range at twelve months in mutual play was from 15 ten-second
blocks to 231 ten-second blocks out of a total of 960 ten-second
blocks of time or from 2-1/2 minutes to 38 minutes during 160
minutes of observation.

One way we have investigated, in attempting to account
for these large differences, is to examine the relationship
between behaviors directed by the infant toward the teachers
and their behaviors directed toward the child. It is not clear
which is the best way to make that comparison. If one simply
sums the behaviors, then frequently occurring behaviors
overwhelm the total. We elected to rank order the infants on
each of six primary social interactive behaviors. By summing
the infant's rank across each of the six behaviors, one can
achieve some determination of how active the infant was compared
to other infants of the same age. Similarly, one can rank order
the infants on each of the behaviors directed by the teachers
toward the infant and achieve a summed rank of how active the
teachers were in initiating interactions with the child. We
correlated these two ranks at each of the ages. Those data
are presented in Table 5.4.

Table 5.4 Rank Order Correlations Comparing Behavior
Directed by and Toward Infants and Teachers at Each of
Three Ages

Teacher Behavior Toward Infants	Infant Behavior Toward Teachers		
	Six Months	Nine Months	Twelve Months
Six months	.60	.40	-.32
	p < .03	NS	NS
Nine months	.73	.78	.15
	p < .003	p < .001	NS
Twelve months	-.008	.16	.27
	NS	NS	NS

    Table 5.4 demonstrates that there was a fairly high corre-
lation between the rank order of infant initiations and the rank
order of teacher initiations at six months and at nine months.
For example, at nine months the correlation is .78 between
behaviors directed by the teachers toward the infants and
behaviors directed by the infants toward the teachers. However, there is no relationship between interactive behaviors of
infants and teachers at twelve months. At twelve months, we
really have no adequate explanation for the great variation
among the infants. It does not appear to be simply a function
of how socially active the infant was.

Attachments Between Particular
Teachers and Infants

    Determination of an attachment relationship is not an easy
task, given that we have no universally accepted criteria. We
chose to investigate the issue in three ways. First, we determined whether and how intensely the infants were making distinctions among the teachers in the amount of their social behavior
directed to the teachers. Second, we investigated the degree
of reciprocity in those preferences. Finally, we looked at the
stability of the preferences across the three ages. If preferential behaviors constituted an attachment "bond" in the classical
sense, we reasoned that they should remain stable, at least
from nine to twelve months.

Differentiation Among the Teachers

The reason we were so careful to attempt to determine to which individual (by name for the five teachers) the child was directing social overtures was that we were interested in the emerging differential relationships one would expect of infants this age. Since it was not clear which of the several attachment behaviors were the important ones for defining a differential relationship in a day care situation, and since the frequency of occurrence was variable across behaviors, we allotted equal weight to all behaviors. For each behavior, teachers were placed in rank order by the number of instances of that behavior that the child directed toward them. The rank orders were then summed across behaviors and a single rank score was determined for each teacher. Thus, if there were six attachment behaviors, the maximum score would be 30 points if one of the five teachers had been top ranked on all six behaviors. A similar procedure was used to score teacher directed behaviors. One could look at individual behaviors or across all six behaviors together to determine the rank order within the group of five teachers in the amount of behavior directed to the child.

The rank order approach described above has limitations: a rank order may obscure very large differences between adjoining ranks in the number of behaviors shown. For example, a child may have directed 64 vocalizations toward the top ranked teacher and only 10 to the second ranked teacher. We tried several approaches to determining preferences by children for teachers and, more importantly, for determining the strength of those preferences. The first was the rank order approach. The second was to use chi square analyses for behaviors where there were enough instances observed to warrant it. However, there tended to be only two behaviors where that was possible: proximity and looking. The other behaviors occurred too infrequently to teachers other than the preferred one.

Table 5.5 depicts the proportion of behaviors directed by the infants at twelve months toward those teachers who by the rank-order approach emerged as the top two teachers of the five. Across the board, nearly 50 percent of the infant's social behaviors are directed toward the single teacher who received a top ranking for the child. Clearly, the ranks are meaningful designations. If behaviors were randomly directed toward the five teachers, then one would expect percentages close to 20 percent for each of the behaviors. (A teacher could, for example, have received a rank of 1 for a child by being the recipient of 21 percent of his or her behaviors if the rest of the behaviors were evenly apportioned among the other teachers.)

Table 5.5 Proportion of Social Behaviors Directed Toward and
Received From Infant's Top-Two Teachers at Twelve Months

| | Infant Directed | | Teacher Directed[a] | |
	First	Second	First	Second
Vocalizations	.527	.207	.509	.242
Play	.572	.242	.572	.242
Touch	.534	.280	.456	.243
Locomotion	.397	.331	—	—
Proximity	.412	.275	.412	.275
Look	.397	.265	.488	.252
Hold	—	—	.418	.271
Total	.473	.266	.476	.254

[a]Behaviors directed toward the infant by those teachers
who were the infant's top two choices.

The second ranked teacher received an average of 27 percent
of the infant's interactive behaviors, so that together two teachers
were eliciting three-quarters of the infant's socially directed
behaviors.

Vocalizations, mutual play, and touching were the behaviors
showing the strongest differentiation among the teachers. That
these behaviors were not simply an accident of location is evident
by the relatively lower proportion attained by proximity as a
separate category.

The first question is then answered in the affirmative—
children were differentiating among the teachers in a day care
setting and, moreover, the intensity of the differentiation was
great.

Reciprocity Between Teachers and Infants

The same procedure which identified the preferred teachers
for the infant was used to investigate differences among the
teachers in the behaviors they showed to a particular infant.
Whereas for the infant we had determined the rank each teacher
attained on behaviors directed by the infant, to determine
reciprocity we ranked the teachers on the behaviors they directed

toward the infant. Which of the teachers, for example, directed the most vocalizations to a particular child? Which played with the infant the most? Which teacher held the child the most? Was there consistency in teacher order across these behaviors? The teacher-preference ranks were then compared to the infant-preference ranks.

At six months, nine of fourteen first-ranks agreed for infants and teachers. Of the five mismatches, three first-ranks by the infants were second-ranked on the teacher orders; two first choices for the infants were third in teacher ranks. At both nine and twelve months, twelve of fourteen first-ranks agreed between infants and teachers. Of the two mismatches at nine months, one was second-ranked and the other third ranked among the teachers, and at twelve months, both mismatches resulted from a first rank being second among teacher ranks. Thus there appeared to be no unrequited love at each age in the day care nursery.

The other important thing to note is that the intensity of discrimination evidenced by the infants was matched by an almost equal intensity among teacher behaviors as is shown in Table 5.5. Note that 50 percent of the vocalizations a twelve month old child received were from the teacher he or she had differentiated as the prime recipient of his or her social behaviors. Overall 73 percent of the social interactions the infant received were from two teachers—those he or she had ranked numbers 1 and 2 by virtue of his or her social initiatives.

We conclude, therefore, that there is much reciprocity between infants and teachers in their social behaviors toward each other. That reciprocity is somewhat evident at six months, more at nine months, and greatly in evidence at twelve months. It is clear that for the twelve month old the social environment of the day care nursery has an order and predictability to it. The infant is not being equally stimulated and approached by all the members of the day care nursery; he or she primarily interacts with a much smaller subset.

Another more tangential question raised by this research is also interesting: the question about whether a single teacher tended to be preferred more than any other. The answer is no. All of the teachers were preferred by individual children. Thus, there was no single attachment figure for all these children.

Stability Across Time

Another way to define the attachment relationship is to determine if these reciprocal relationships evidenced at each age are stable across time since at least one previous study of attachment in polymatric situations has used stability as a hall-mark of attachment (Stevens, 1971).

The answer is simple: almost no stability was evidenced across the three ages. Four children maintained the same top ranked teacher from six to twelve months. The greatest insta-bility was between nine and twelve months. There, the only children maintaining the same top rank across the ages were those four previously mentioned. All others changed, and moreover they changed in unpredictable ways. For three of the infants, the teacher who had been ranked last at nine months became the top ranked teacher at twelve months. That this was a meaningful and dramatic shift is evidenced by the fact that at all ages top ranked teachers were receiving and initiating 70 percent of the social interactions just as we described at twelve months. These dramatic shifts did not occur between six and nine months. Eight children maintained their top rank from one age to the other, and no teacher moved dramatically up in rank.

We have no obvious explanation for either why the shift occurred at twelve months or why it did not occur at nine months. For normally developing children at home, we expect to see the strongest emergence of attachment beginning at nine months and peaking at twelve months (Schaffer and Emerson, 1964). We did notice that certain teachers tended to show up more frequently at certain ages, indicating perhaps that they responded to particular ages more than others. It could be that much of the reciprocity at six and nine months was deter-mined more by teacher preference than by infant preference. As the infant became more mobile and more vocal, it is possible that the preferences became more independent of teacher initia-tive, in other words, that the burden of the relationship shifted from teacher to infant between six and twelve months.

The idea of an attachment bond raises the issue of how adaptive such a bond would actually be in a day care environ-ment. It may, in fact, be maladaptive in a group situation to form a strong, exclusive attachment relationship with one teacher. There is no question that the infant will have to share that caregiver's attention with others, and to protest that sharing of attention would be highly disruptive. In a polymatric situation, adaptability to different caregivers, perhaps with a reciprocal preference for one or two, may be the most adaptive procedure for the infant to follow. It is interesting that the infants do protest caregiving by visitors in the nursery other than the regular teachers, most clearly shown by the inability of a visitor to comfort a distressed infant.

DISCUSSION

These observations suggest a social system in the day care nursery whereby teachers and infants are continually sorting themselves into preferred patterns of interacting. These shifting allegiances make the day care center a very different social environment from the home where, even if parent and child have very dissimilar personalities and tempos, they must remain together and work out some pattern of interacting which is mutually acceptable. Although the behavioral patterns between infants and teachers seem to be very intense and even exclusive, the fact that they do not persist across time removes them from consideration as true attachment relationships, in our opinion.

The lack of formation of true attachment bonds to day care teachers is not necessarily negative, although there are those who have asserted to the contrary (Anderson et al., 1981). It does demonstrate that for children who come from chaotic, disrupted homes where there may be a problem developing an attachment relationship, the day care nursery will not provide an adequate substitute.

Day care environments are ones which constantly change. Children move in and out; teachers are sick; substitutes replace them for days; other teachers leave, often precipitously. Most group day care situations would be far more unstable than most homes. Attempting to chart interactions in a setting like that is prone to problems. For example, the oldest children in our study actually experienced a different environment from those who entered later—there were fewer teachers and children present. Although this seems like a methodological problem, it is an insoluble one, because change is a fact of life in a day care nursery. All of these children left the nursery when they were between thirteen to eighteen months old and went to new classrooms with different teachers—a radical change for all.

There are two additional questions raised by this set of observations. The first relates to the level of play observed between teachers and infants. Given that sleeping, caregiving, and eating take up a not insignificant portion of the day and that we were observing "play" time, mutual play with an adult for less than 10 percent of the time seems worthy of further attention. Fowler (1975) made the point forcefully:

> The core of the problem [in infant day care] is the
> finite availability of adult energy and the distribu-
> tion of adult attention. Competence and motivation

can only go so far in organizing the distribution of
attention. Beyond certain optimum ratio levels
appropriate for each age, every child added to the
denominator of the adult/child care ratio necessarily
further divides the amount of attention among more
children and dilutes the adult attention every child
receives whether measured in terms of separate
single interactions or in terms of the distribution
of adult attention in small groups (Fowler, 1975,
pg. 25).

A further question relates to the fact that some children
received much less attention than the average would suggest.
There were striking individual differences among the infants
in this group in terms of the qualtity of their interactions with
adults. The question to be pursued further is whether that
difference has any long term significance for the infant and,
if so, in what ways. It could be that these differences affect
the comfort or happiness the child is experiencing at the time,
but that unless these patterns are repeated with other teachers
in subsequent classrooms, they are without much consequence.
However, before we can be sanguine about the variation, we
ought to determine whether, in fact, there are consequences.
Let us conclude with an anecdote which illustrates the
social world of a day care nursery where children ranged in
age from one and one-half to fifteen months and how that
narrow age range begins to affect one's perspective. Two
infants were playing with the same toy, one of whom was the
target child for our observations. Two of us were taking
reliability data. As the data demonstrated, peer interactions
in mutual play were relatively rare. Thus we were delighted
to be observing this twelve month old playing together with
an eight month old. One observer grinned at the other, whisper-
ing, "Aren't they cute?" As the other observer smiled, the
first then said quickly (and seriously), "But, of course, he
is much too old for her." In terms of skills, perhaps indeed
he was. It is unlikely, however, that a four month age difference will be important for long.

REFERENCES

Ainsworth, M. D. The development of infant-mother attachment.
In B. Caldwell and H. Ricciuti (Eds.), Review of child de-
velopment research (Vol. 3). Chicago: University of Chicago
Press, 1973.

Anderson, C. W., Nagle, R. J., Roberts, W. A., and Smith,
    J. W. Attachment to substitute caregivers as a function of
    center quality and caregiver involvement. Child Development,
    1981, 52, 53-61.

Farran, D., and Ramey, C. Infant day care and attachment
    behaviors toward mothers and teachers. Child Development,
    1977, 48, 1112-1116.

Fein, G., and Clarke-Stewart, A. Day care in context. New
    York: John Wiley & Sons, 1973.

Fowler, W. How adult/child ratios influence infant development.
    Interchange, 1975, 6, 17-31.

Kagan, J., Kearsley, R. B., and Zelazo, P. R. The effects
    of infant day care on psychological development. Presented
    at the symposium "The Effect of Early Experience on Child
    Development." American Association for the Advancement
    of Science, February, 1976, Boston, MA.

Krentz, M. Qualitative differences between mother-child and
    caregiver-child attachments of infants in family day care.
    Paper presented at the biennial meeting of the Society for
    Research in Child Development, Detroit, April 1983.

McCall, R. B., and Appelbaum, M. E. Bias in the analysis
    of repeated-measures designs: Some alternative approaches.
    Child Development, 1973, 44, 401-415.

Rutter, M. Social-emotional consequences of day care for
    preschool children. American Journal of Orthopsychiatry,
    1981, 51, 4-28.

Schaffer, H. R., and Emerson, P. E. The development of
    social attachments in infancy. Monographs of the Society
    for Research in Child Development, Vol. 29, No. 3, 1964.

Stevens, A. G. Attachment behaviour, separation anxiety,
    and stranger anxiety in polymatrically reared infants. In
    H. R. Schaffer (Ed.), The origins of human social relations.
    London: Academic Press, 1971.

Wilcox, B., Staff, P., and Romaine, M. A comparison of
    individual and multiple assignment of caregivers to infants

in daycare. Unpublished paper, Zale Learning Center, Dallas, Texas; undated.

$$\text{----------------------------} 6. \text{----------------------------}$$

Toward a Model of Infant Day Care: Studies of Factors Influencing Responding to Separation in Day Care

E. Mark Cummings and Jessica Beagles-Ross

In most day care research it has been assumed that day care is a relatively simple environment with a single set of effects associated with it (Anderson, 1980). The thrust of research has been to determine whether day care is good or bad for children. In reality, this question is probably un-answerable. Day care is a very complex environment and is likely to have complex sets of effects on children. The problem for day care research is not to determine whether day care is good or bad, but to determine the elements of good versus inadequate or undesirable day care (Zaslow, Rabinovich, and Suwalsky, in press).

In order to proceed in this, one must break day care down into its component parts and examine how each exercises an effect on children's development in day care. Figure 6.1 presents a framework for conceptualizing these factors. One important set of influences is brought to the day care system by the child. In a sense, the child brings a type of influence from the home; the emotional security infants internalize from parents for going into new environments and the continuity versus discontinuity which exist between the roles and values of the two systems (Long, Garduque, and Peters, 1983) may

Acknowledgments. We would like to thank Christine Dimond and Maureen Kelly for their assistance in data decoding and analysis. We are grateful to Marian Radke-Yarrow for her comments on an earlier draft of this paper.

159

Figure 6.1 Influences on Development in Day Care

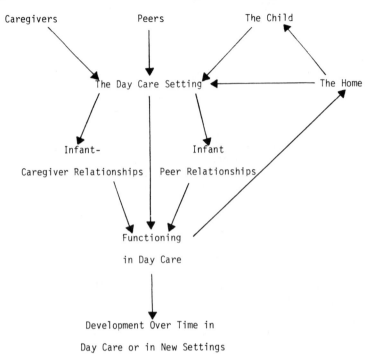

each affect functioning in day care. Parents may also influence
adaptation to day care by their behavior during entry to or
departure from day care. For example, parental anxiety about
separation can increase children's distress during this period
(Hock, this volume), which may carry over into the rest of the
day. Other influences are linked to the child's sex, age, or
other characteristics. There is evidence that variations in
these are associated with variation in the effect of day care on
children (see review in Rutter, 1981). Another set of effects
associated with the individual child may be attributable to the
child's basic disposition or temperament. Highly active or,
alternatively, withdrawn and fearful children might be expected
to have the greatest difficulty with separation or interaction
in a group setting. A problem for research on this issue is
that it is not well-understood how to conceptualize individual
differences in what the child is like emotionally; there is a lack
of consensus regarding the definition of temperament (Goldsmith
and Campos, 1982). Finally, day care outcomes may be influenced by previous experience in day care and the nature of

that experience; how long the child has attended day care
(Blanchard and Main, 1979); the intensity of the day care
experience (how many hours per day) (Schwartz, 1983) and
the age at which the child entered day care (Howes and Rubenstein, 1983; McCartney et al., 1982; Moskowitz, Schwarz, and
Corsini, 1977; Portnoy and Simmons, 1978; Schwartz, Krolick,
and Strickland, 1973; Vaughn, Gove, and Egeland, 1980).

The other individuals in the day care setting also are
sources of influence on development in day care. Caregivers
can differ on a number of dimensions: their past training,
their sensitivity to child development issues, their personality,
their socioeconomic status background. Each of these may
affect their interactions with children in day care. Peers constitute another set of influences. Each peer can vary on as
many characteristics as the target child. Thus, the complexity
of peers as an influence can be great. Factors associated with
the individual characteristics of caregivers and peers have been
neglected in research as influences on development in day care.

Over time, relationships may develop between children
and caregivers or between children and other children. These
relationships can come to have an influence of their own,
distinct from the individual characteristics of children or caregivers. The formation of infant-caregiver attachments (Ainslie
and Anderson, 1982; Anderson et al., 1981; Cummings, 1980;
Krentz, 1983; Ricciuti, 1974) could significantly affect infant-
caregiver relations. On the basis of attachment research
(Ainsworth et al., 1978), it would be expected that infant-
caregiver relations would be positively influenced by the
formation of attachments, particularly if attachments were
secure. In terms of peers, friendships with peers might be
important to the quality of the child's experience in day care.
This issue has been largely uninvestigated. Furthermore, the
peer system itself might form relationships (dominance hier-
archies or affiliative structures) which could influence development in day care (Strayer, 1980, 1981; Strayer and Noel, in
press).

Turning to the day care center itself, the characteristics
of the setting may also contribute to the quality of the child's
experience in day care. Among the potentially significant
elements of the day care setting are the physical characteristics
of the setting, the number of toys and how the space is organized, group size (Howes and Rubenstein, 1983; Travers and
Ruopp, 1978), teacher roles (Rubenstein and Howes, 1979),
caregiver-child ratio (Howes and Rubenstein, 1983; Travers
and Ruopp, 1978), caregiver stability (Cummings, 1980), and

the rules and values of the center for dealing with children,
e.g., discipline and rearing practices. The characteristics
of the day care setting may affect the quality of the child's
exploration and play, and act to structure infants' interactions
with others in the center, having both an immediate impact on
these interactions, and, over time, an effect on the development
of relationships with others. Rubrics for conceptualizing the
physical setting have been suggested by Peterson (see Anderson et al., 1981), and Prescott et al. (1975).

These variables can be seen as pieces in a puzzle that
need to be put together in order to understand and predict
relationships between attendance in day care and socioemotional
development. As the figure illustrates, relationships may be
complex; variables may interact with each other in influencing
development.

Adding another level of complexity to this picture, for
each dimension of development that is influenced by attendance
in day care there may be different interrelationships between
variables. Accordingly, given the research effort likely to be
required to understand even a single element of functioning,
the focus should be on non-trivial outcomes. Conceptually
significant categories that may be linked with early day care
include behavior problems (Schwarz, Strickland, and Krolick,
1974; Finkelstein, 1982), children's relations with parents
(Blehar, 1974), and socialization patterns (see review in Bronfenbrenner, 1979).

Day care may also have effects which extend beyond the
day care setting (Belsky, 1980; Belsky and Steinberg, 1978;
Bronfenbrenner, 1979). For young children there is likely to
be an interactive relationship between development in the home
and development in day care. For example, patterns of emotional
bonding and socialization may mutually influence each other.
Immediate functioning in day care may also have implications
for later functioning in day care and for adaptation to new
environments; outcomes which have been neglected in day care
research (Belsky and Steinberg, 1978; Frye, 1982; Rutter, 1981).

The model presented in Figure 6.1 thus serves as a guide
for research. The research presented below illustrates this
model in addressing relationships between variables from within
and outside day care and responding to a particular element of
day care experience: separation from the parents in the day
care environment.

DAY CARE SEPARATIONS AND INFANTS'
FELT-SECURITY

Day care separations are, in themselves, a significant
setting for observing infants' emotional functioning in day care.
They are likely to be among the most stressful events in the
child's day; it is thus important to determine which factors
optimize children's ability to cope. In addition, responses to
day care separations may have implications for functioning in
day care which extend beyond the separation context itself.
From a broader perspective, day care separations can be seen
as a context for observing infants' felt-security in day care,
and factors influencing responses to day care separations can
be interpreted as affecting infants' general felt-security in day
care.

The model outlined in Figure 6.1 provides both a general
guide for conceptualizing interrelationships between variables
in the day care setting, and can be used as a rubric for investigating factors influencing specific developmental functions, or
behavior in specific contexts. In the present instance, we use
it as a framework for considering factors influencing felt-security
in day care, as indicated by behavior during day care separations. While felt-security is typically thought of in terms of
infant-parent attachments within the day care setting, the
infants' sense of security may also be a function of interpersonal
relationships with caregivers and peers and responses to the
physical environment. Further, factors which influence responding to these elements of day care may act as mediating influences.

Behavior in the day care setting may provide a more
reliable index of influences on development in day care than
generalizations based upon behavior in other contexts. Cummings (1980) reported sharp differences between responding
to day care caregivers in the laboratory and in the home. In
the laboratory, infants tended to become distressed when left
with caregivers and frequently searched for the mother after
her departure. In the day care setting the same children seldom
either searched for the mother or cried. Thus, the security
provided by caregivers in day care may be underestimated by
behavior in outside settings. There could be some points of
correspondence, however. Blanchard and Main (1979) found
that avoidance of the mother during reunion in day care and
in the Strange Situation was of comparable magnitude, and
there was a positive correlation between avoidance scores in
the two settings.

FACTORS WITHIN THE DAY CARE SETTING
AS INFLUENCES ON RESPONDING TO
DAY CARE SEPARATIONS

As Figure 6.1 illustrates, infant-caregiver interactions may be influenced by the characteristics of the day care setting. In the research reported below, we examine caregiver stability and group size as influences on felt-security during day care separations.

Research on maternal deprivation, separation, and attachment suggest that stability has a positive influence on the development of infant-adult relationships. In addition, it has been argued in the day care literature that greater caregiver stability should improve the quality of infant-adult relationships in day care (Anderson, 1980; Belsky, 1980; Fein and Clarke-Stewart, 1973; Frye, 1982; Provence, 1974), and several day care studies relevant to stability have been conducted (see below). However, within-child tests of caregiver stability (comparisons of responding to stable versus nonstable caregivers for the same child) have seldom been conducted. This provides the best-controlled test of stability as a distinct factor. When comparisons are made between children, other differences between the life experiences of children, e.g., separations, or conflict in the home, may influence results.

Caregiver stability can be thought of in terms of continuity over time or in terms of the intensity of daily infant-adult association. Day care research suggests that continuity positively influences both infant and caregiver functioning in day care. Moore (1975) reported that the number of different substitute caregiving regimes experienced before the age of five (one or two versus three or more) predicted sleeping problems, dependence upon maternal affection, nail biting, attention and help seeking at home, and emotional support needs in the center at age six. However, since comparison groups also differed on other characteristics, it is uncertain whether results reflect differences in continuity or other differences between families (Rutter, 1981). Rubenstein, Pedersen, and Yarrow (1977) found that the duration of regular contact between infants and substitute caregivers was positively related to caregivers' expressions of positive affect to the infant, talking to the infant, contingent response to distress, and contingent vocalization. Rubenstein and Howes (1979) reported that twice as much interaction took place in day care between infants and head teachers as between infants and volunteers. Head teachers and volunteers differed on continuity: Head teachers had been

with children since entry into day care, but volunteers had
changed since that time. However, the impact of continuity
was modified by the roles of teachers in day care. Assistant
teachers were equivalent to head teachers in terms of continuity,
but their pattern of interaction with infants did not differ from
volunteers. Thus, caregiver stability and teacher roles appeared
to interact in influencing outcomes.

The intensity of daily infant-caregiver association can be
thought of as the time infants and caregivers spend interacting
each day, or, more simply, as the time they are in the same
environment together. The significance of the amount of time
infants and caregivers spend interacting has been addressed
in several studies, although it has not been conceptualized in
precisely this manner; and the results are far from conclusive.
Anderson et al. (1981) examined the importance of caregiver
involvement, which can be seen as an index of daily contact.
They found that high caregiver involvement was associated with
greater contact seeking, distance interaction, and exploratory
behaviors in the presence of caregivers in the Strange Situation.
Children in high caregiver involvement/high physical quality
groups evidenced the greatest attachment behavior to caregivers;
providing another instance in which elements of the day care
setting appeared to interact. Continuity was largely controlled;
all children had been in the continuous care of the same caregiver for at least eight months. However, since comparisons
were made across centers, comparison groups could have also
differed on other characteristics. Wilcox, Staff, and Romaine
(1980) investigated a dimension of day care settings—individual
versus multiple assignments of caregivers to infants—which
could be related to daily contact. They found no differences
in the total amount of social contact with caregivers, or in
behavior during separation or reunion in the two settings, but
it is uncertain whether this comparison effectively manipulated
daily interaction, because social behavior toward the assigned
caregiver in the individual assignment center and toward the
most primary caregiver in the multiple assignment center did
not differ. No studies looking exclusively at the importance of
the amount of time spent by children and caregivers in the
same environment have been conducted.

Cummings (1980) defined stability in terms of the total
hours of coincident attendance of infants and caregivers in
day care, and responses to stable and nonstable caregivers
during separation were compared. Infants were less resistant
to transfer from the mother to stable caregivers upon entry
and evidenced greater positive affect following separation from

the mother when left with stable caregivers. However, this stability criterion combined continuity over time and time together each day, and so does not address their separate significance.

To summarize, research suggests that continuity over time positively influences infant-caregiver relations in day care, whereas daily association is of less certain import. However, these issues are still largely unexplored, and only two studies have compared responding to stable versus nonstable caregivers for the same children (Cummings, 1980; Rubenstein and Howes, 1979). In the analyses below, Cummings' (1980) data are reanalyzed so that continuity over time and daily association are distinguished. This study provides both within-child analyses of these dimensions of stability and the first examination of the significance of the intensity of daily association defined exclusively in terms of the amount of time infants and caregivers spent in the same environment together.

Group size is another element of the day care setting that may influence infants' functioning in day care. Travers and Ruopp (1978) found that among three to five year olds, caregivers engaged in more interaction in smaller groups, and children generally were more interested and active participants. In a study of toddlers, Howes and Rubenstein (1983) reported that children in both family and center day care had higher talk scores in smaller groups, but there were no differences in caregiver behavior. In the present study, the issue of the effect of group size on functioning in day care is extended to day care separations.

Finally, while distinct effects associated with these elements of the day care environment are anticipated, interactions might also be expected, consistent with the present model and previous research on relationships between dimensions of the day care setting.

A STUDY OF CAREGIVER STABILITY AND GROUP SIZE AS INFLUENCES ON RESPONDING TO DAY CARE SEPARATIONS

The subjects were 30 children between one and two and one-half years of age ($\bar{X}$ = 21.7 months) attending two day care centers serving UCLA students and staff. All had begun day care in infancy ($\bar{X}$ = 10.5 months) and had been in day care for at least two months prior to participation in the study ($\bar{X}$ = 10.4 months). Most were in full time care (at least 30 hours per week).

The group size at Center A averaged 20 to 25 infants, whereas the group size at Center B averaged 8 to 12 infants. In other respects the centers were comparable. Both centers had caregiver-child ratios of about 4:1, and experienced staff. Caregivers were not assigned to specific infants but shared in the care of all children.

Stable and nonstable caregivers were chosen to be tested with each child on the basis of attendance records. Only one dimension of infant-caregiver association--intensity of daily association or continuity over time—varied for each pairing (see Cummings, 1978, for more information on caregiver assignments).

Seventeen children (ten boys and seven girls) were observed with caregivers who differed in the intensity of daily association. Stable caregivers had worked in the center an average 73 percent of the child's day since first meeting the child, whereas nonstable caregivers had worked an average 38 percent of the child's day; but caregivers differed little on continuity of association (8.5 versus 8.2 months, respectively).

Thirteen children (eight boys and five girls) were observed with caregivers who differed on continuity. In this condition, stable caregivers had been in the center with children for a mean of 9.8 months, whereas nonstable caregivers had been with children for 2.5 months; but the difference in terms of the intensity of their association each day was slight (43 percent versus 38 percent of the child's day).

To reduce the influence of teacher characteristics, twelve adults served as caregivers, and five alternated between stable and nonstable caregiver roles. To insure caregivers were not strangers, all had been in the center for at least one month prior to observations.

Children were observed as they were dropped off at the day care center on two separate days. On one day the mother specifically left the child with the stable caregiver, whereas on the other the child was left with the nonstable caregiver. The only instruction given to mothers was that they transfer the child to the assigned caregiver just before entering the center. Caregivers were asked to take the child from the mother at the door, and stay with the child until two minutes after the mother left. Episodes averaged five minutes and seventeen seconds. Responses were recorded by a hand-held video camera.

In describing responses to separations, we wished to characterize the infants' general emotional well-being, their specific reactions to reunion with caregivers at the center,

their interactions with caregivers, and, as a further character-
ization of relationships with caregivers, the tendency to stay
with the assigned caregiver versus seeking contact with the
mother both before and after separation. Specifically, the
variables recorded were (unless otherwise noted, measurement
is in seconds): (a) Negative affect before and after separation—
crying, cry face, wary brow, eyes wide or down, (b) Positive
affect before and after separation—active or quiet smiles, (c)
Avoidance during entry into the center--refusing to enter the
center, stalling during entry, or turning or backing away
from the center, (d) Rating of resistance during physical
transfer from mother to caregiver—rated on a 3-point scale
from no resistance to active resistance, (e) Infant-caregiver
interaction—verbal interaction or interaction during play,
(f) Orientation to mother before separation—frequencies of
looking at the mother when in proximity to the caregiver or
moving toward the mother and away from the caregiver, (g)
Proximity to the mother before separation—staying near the
mother rather than the caregiver, and (h) Searching for the
mother after separation—looking at where the mother had been
or moving after the mother as she leaves. Pearson product-
moment interobserver reliability coefficients for these measures
ranged from .90 to 1.00 (X = .96).

Time Together Each Day (Intensity Condition)

The means and results are shown in Table 6.1. Variables
were analyzed by one within (more versus less intense caregivers) X one between (smaller versus larger group size)
subjects analyses of variance. There were no significant main
effects or interactions for intensity of association.

Continuity Over Time

Table 6.1 also presents the findings for this condition.
Continuity X group size ANOVAs were performed. Continuity
positively influenced responding: Children were less resistant
of physical reunion with more continuous caregivers, and were
less likely to leave the caregiver and seek proximity with the
mother. In addition, general emotional functioning was better
following separation when children were left with more continuous
caregivers. Children exhibited less separation distress with
more continuous caregivers, and were also more likely to smile

Table 6.1 Caregiver Stability and Response to Day Care Separations

Criteria for Stability

Response	Time Together Each Day			Continuity Over Time		
	Stable Caregiver	Nonstable Caregiver	Significance of Difference	Stable Caregiver	Nonstable Caregiver	Significance of Difference
Avoidance During Entry	2.5	1.7	NS	1.2	3.9	NS
Resistance to Caregiver	1.5	1.9	NS	1.2	2.0	.05
Infant-Caregiver Interaction	67.9	67.9	NS	72.1	83.2	NS
Orientation to Mother	3.9	3.7	NS	2.2	2.4	NS
Proximity to Mother	46.2	31.9	NS	3.2	20.5	.01
Preseparation Positive Affect	8.5	13.5	NS	10.9	12.5	NS
Preseparation Negative Affect	29.5	18.1	NS	19.1	27.5	NS
Postseparation Search	2.1	6.1	NS	1.5	1.1	NS
Postseparation Positive Affect	7.2	5.5	NS	13.4	4.8	.05
Postseparation Negative Affect	14.9	7.4	NS	6.9	15.9	.05

or laugh in the period immediately following the mothers departure.

Group Size

Children from the center characterized by smaller group size fared consistently better during day care separations. In analyses of the time together each day as an element of caregiver stability, children from the smaller center showed more positive affect prior to separation ($p < .05$), and less avoidance during entry ($p < .10$). In the continuity condition, children from the smaller center spent less time searching for the mother following separation ($p < .05$). There was also an interaction between group size and continuity of association for postseparation positive affect ($p < .05$). Children responded with considerably greater positive affect in the postseparation when left with more continuous caregivers in the larger center, $p < .05$, but there was little difference in responding in the smaller center.

As the model in Figure 6.1 predicts, programmatic elements of the day care setting influenced felt-security as indicated by responses to day care separations. Responses were in part a function of the stability of infant-caregiver association. However, the patterning of infant-caregiver association was clearly critical to its significance to infants' felt-security. Despite the fact that the continuity and intensity conditions involved almost equivalent manipulations of coincident attendance, continuity had a notable impact on responding whereas intensity did not. These results add to a growing child development literature which suggests that, while continuity is of considerable significance to infant-adult relations (e.g., see Bowlby, 1976, on separation and child development), the amount of daily association is of much lesser import (e.g., see Zaslow et al., in press, on maternal employment and child development). However, while daily exposure might not be significant, daily contact may merit further investigation (see Anderson et al., 1981).

More broadly, the findings suggest that infant-caregiver attachments are positively influenced by continuity. The variables on which infants responded more favorably with more continuous caregivers—reactions to reunion, selectivity in proximity seeking, and separation affect—each reflect quality of attachment (Ainsworth et al., 1978; Cohen, 1974).

Group size also influenced responding. Smaller group size was associated with responses indicative of greater felt-security. The results add further support to the notion that day care children function better in smaller group settings.

Finally, caregiver stability and group size also had inter-active effects, as expected. Higher quality in one element of the day care setting, i.e., greater caregiver stability, appeared to be more important when another element was of lower quality, i.e., larger group size.

FACTORS FROM OUTSIDE THE DAY CARE SETTING
AND FROM WITHIN THE CHILD AS INFLUENCES
ON RESPONDING TO DAY CARE SEPARATIONS

As Figure 6.1 illustrates, the home and the child each might also be expected to influence functioning in day care. This second study examines the relative roles of the father and mother and individual differences in infants' response patterns as factors in felt-security during day care separations.

As the figure shows, there is likely to be an interactive relationship between development in day care and in the home. Research on interrelationships between these environments has focused on the effects of day care on infants' attachments to parents. The central questions have been: (a) Does day care disrupt attachment relations with the mother? and (b) Do day care caregivers replace the mother as infants' primary attachment figures? As several reviewers have noted (see Belsky and Steinberg, 1978; Rutter, 1981), the evidence suggests that, although day care may be associated with dis-ruption in infant-mother attachment, it does not necessarily interfere. There is no evidence that day care caregivers come to replace the mother as infants' primary attachment figures. The mother has been found to remain a more primary attachment figure, even in situations in which caregivers and mothers have had roughly equal exposure to children since early infancy (Farran and Ramey, 1977).

Until recently, however, the effect of the home on function-ing in day care had not been considered. Secure infant-parent attachments should facilitate bonding with caregivers in day care, since securely attached children are more positive, out-going, and sociable in their relations with others (Main and Weston, 1981; Pastor, 1981; Waters, Wippman, and Sroufe, 1979). Consistent with this prediction, Ainslie and Anderson (1982) reported a significant positive association between the security of attachments to mothers and caregivers, but Krentz (1983) found these attachments were independent. Attachments to the father may also influence infants' security in day care. Chibucos and Chibucos (1983) reported that the security of attachment to the father was positively correlated with adjustment and social skills in day care. However, since infant-father and infant-mother attachments were positively correlated, this might reflect the combined influence of attachments in the home.

While research is beginning to examine the significance of infant-parent relationships to functioning in day care, there are no studies comparing the effectiveness of parents when both parents and children are together in the day care setting itself, i.e., during day care separations and reunions. More generally, the security provided by parents may be better demonstrated by responses to separation in day care than by responses in other settings. This avoids problems of ecological validity and generalizability associated with laboratory attachment tests which have been conducted on this issue.

Attention has recently been called to the individual child as a factor in how infants respond and function in day care (Howe and Rubenstein, 1983). However, there have been few demonstrations of the role played by the child. Tests of consistency over time and across separations involving the same adults are biased because stabilities peculiar to specific infant-adult interaction patterns can figure in results. A more conservative test examines consistency in responding across separations when the identities of adults change. In the present paper, we examine stabilities across separations when either the caregiver or the parent is changed.

A STUDY OF PARENTAL IDENTITY AND CHILD CONSISTENCY AS INFLUENCES ON RESPONDING TO DAY CARE SEPARATIONS

The subjects were ten boys and six girls and were a subsample of the children referred to in Study 1. Subjects failed to participate in the present study either because the father was unavailable or unwilling to be videotaped leaving the child at the day center (N = 13) or because the mother was a single parent (N = 1). The mean age of this group of children at the onset of their participation in this study was 19.3 months.

Children were observed as they were left at the day care center by their parents on four separate days. On two occasions the parent dropping the child off was the mother while on the other two occasions the parent leaving the child was the father. Each parent left the child with the designated stable caregiver on one occasion and with the designated nonstable caregiver on the other. Thus, the following combinations of parents and caregivers were observed on different days: mother-stable caregiver, mother-nonstable caregiver, father-stable caregiver, and father-nonstable caregiver.

Two new measures were added to index the role of parental behavior in day care separations: (a) Time of parents' stay and (b) Good-bye at separation—whether the parent said good-bye before leaving the center. Each may indirectly indicate the parents' anxiety at separation.

Mother- Versus Father-Mediated Separations

Analyses of variance with one within-subject factor (father versus mother) and one between-subject factor (children's sex) were conducted; results are shown in Table 6.2. Separations from parents differed in several respects. Children evidenced greater positive affect with fathers prior to separation but searched more for mothers after separation. Mothers also spent more time in the center than fathers prior to separation. No significant sex main effects were obtained, but there was a significant parent × sex interaction for negative affect after separation (p < .05). Boys were more distressed than girls following separation from the mother, Tukey, p < .05, but boys and girls responded similarly to separation from the father.

Consistencies in Responding Across Day Care Separations

Correlations across separations were calculated: (a) as a function of change in the identity of caregivers, i.e., the two stable versus the two nonstable caregiver separations, and (b) as a function of change in the identity of parents, i.e., the two mother versus the two father separations. Results are presented in Table 6.3. There were high positive correlations for most variables, but more correlations were significant when the identity of parents changed. Greatest consistency was evident for general emotional functioning during day care separations; the eight correlations reported ranged from .38 to .75. Correlations for resistance to physical contact with

Table 6.2 Parent Identity and Responses to Day Care
Separations

Behavior	Parent		Significance of Difference
	Father	Mother	
Avoidance During Entry	5.9	3.1	NS
Resistance to Caregiver	1.7	1.6	NS
Infant-Caregiver Interaction	53.4	67.7	NS
Orientation to Parent	3.8	3.3	NS
Parent	25.7	29.0	NS
Preseparation Positive Affect	20.6	10.1	.05
Preseparation Negative Affect	24.9	31.8	NS
Postseparation Search	.2	2.1	.05
Postseparation Positive Affect	11.6	6.8	NS
Postseparation Negative Affect	11.3	15.4	NS
Parents Stay in Center	186.2	230.4	.05
Percent Good-bye at Separation	.75	.75	NS

Table 6.3 Consistencies in Responding Across Separations
When Selected Adults Change

Response	Adult Changed			
	Caregiver	Significance	Parent	Significance
Avoidance During Entry	.49	$p < .05$	.23	NS
Resistance to Caregiver	.62	$p < .01$	.66	$p < .01$
Infant-Caregiver Interaction	-.13	NS	.31	NS
Orientation to Parent	.38	NS	.53	$p < .05$
Proximity to Parent	-.09	NS	.79	$p < .01$
Preseparation Positive Affect	.44	NS	.75	$p < .01$
Preseparation Negative Affect	.59	$p < .05$	.64	$p < .01$
Postseparation Search	-.28	NS	-.08	NS
Postseparation Positive Affect	.38	NS	.58	$p < .05$
Postseparation Negative Affect	.40	NS	.64	$p < .01$

All values are Pearson product-moment correlations.

174

caregivers were also high: .62 and .66. The least consistent categories were infant-caregiver interaction and post-separation search (all NS).

Children responded differently to father- and mother-mediated separations. However, this does not necessarily indicate differences in the security derived from parents. Responding to parents was far more similar than dissimilar. Greater positive affect with fathers prior to separation could reflect differences in infant-parent interaction styles rather than differences in felt-security. Greater playfulness has been found generally to characterize infant-father interactions (Lamb, 1976b, 1976c), and this could result in more smiling or laughing when with the father. While children had more difficulty separating from the mother, as indicated by more search for her after she left, mothers could have been more anxious than fathers about leaving children, and may have behaved in such a way as to elicit separation reactions. Hock (this volume) has found a positive association between mothers' anxiety at separation and separation distress. In the present study, mothers took longer to complete day care separations; this could indicate they were more reluctant to or anxious about separating. The greater separation distress among boys with the mother suggests that, whatever the source of greater difficulty in leave-taking from the mother, boys were more vulnerable, consistent with other research on day care effects (see review in Rutter, 1981). To put these results in perspective, however, these differences, while significant, were small (particularly the difference for postseparation search).

Consistency analyses suggest that individual children tend to respond in the same way, despite changes in the identity of the adults involved. This affirms the importance of the set of influences brought to the day care system by the child, but does not distinguish between them. It remains for future research to determine the critical influences in molding the child's ongoing sense of felt-security. Individual differences are particularly evident with regard to general emotional adaptation to and avoidance of day care. The higher incidence of significant correlations when the identity of parents rather than caregivers was changed could reflect greater similarity in patterns of attachment to parents, and also suggests that the identity of the caregiver may be more important than the identity of parents to responding to day care separations.

GENERAL DISCUSSION

The findings support the central hypotheses of the present model: (a) responding to day care is a function of multivariate elements from both within and outside the day care system and (b) more specifically, felt-security during day care separations is a function of interpersonal relationships with caregivers and responses to the more general day care setting, i.e., group size, as well as a function of infant-parent attachments. Group size could mediate infant-caregiver relationships. Infant inter-actions with caregivers were generally facilitated by smaller group size. However, greater caregiver stability made more of a difference to responding in larger groups. Greater stability may compensate for less propitious social settings.

The complexity of influences on felt-security in day care is indicated. Day care separations can be viewed as "reunions" with day care. Parallels can be seen between behavior during day care separations and responses to reunion in the Strange Situation (Ainsworth et al., 1978). In both instances, response patterns tend to be consistent over time, but are sensitive to a variety of influences. The treatment of factors likely to influence felt-security is far from complete. In addition, even when considered most broadly, the results only pertain to influences on infants' sense of emotional well-being in day care. Different patterns of relationships might be obtained in studies of socialization outcomes, or patterns of general social and emotional interaction with peers and caregivers. Contexts other than day care separations may be more appropriate to the study of other issues.

The present research highlights the need for researchers to be more sophisticated in their consideration of day care as a problem for research. The issue is not simply a polemic: To prove day care is good or bad for infants. This view is both useless from a social policy perspective; the need for out-of-home care for infants will continue to be an inevitable byproduct of changes in economic conditions and parents' roles (Hildebrand, 1982), and is an oversimplified and inaccurate theoretical model of day care. Researchers must face the fact that day care requires innovative and complex model building and clear research designs to be understood (the present work is only a rudimentary start on this road). On the other hand, the payoffs fully merit the investment. Much of the coming generation may be reared, at least in part, in day care settings during early and developmentally formative years.

We can offer some suggestions with regard to the practical issue of carrying out this research. One strategy for research

is to sample from many different levels of the day care system
at the same time, allowing a broad overview both of the relative
significance of factors within the day care setting, and of
interrelationships between variables. The present research
illustrates a second tack, focusing in-depth on a few elements
of the day care system. This approach potentially allows for
greater experimental control. In the present research, for
example, the within-subject design controlled child-related
variability in assessing caregiver stability and parental identity
as factors influencing responding to day care separations.

Broad-scale and narrow-focused research strategies ideally
should be used in concert. However, results for a single study
will inevitably be dependent upon the specific setting investigated.
In particular, interrelationships between variables may change
with change in the relative salience of target factors. Ultimately,
functional relationships within the day care system will only
become clear as an outgrowth of studies in a variety of settings
and with a variety of populations. The pattern of findings is
likely to be complex in their complete detail. From a practical
perspective, it can be hoped that a small number of factors
ultimately will emerge as critical to day care quality. This is
only likely to occur, however, from an exhaustive investigation
of the interrelationships within the day care system.

REFERENCES

Ainslie, R. C., and Anderson, C. W. Caregiver-infant inter-
    action in the day care setting and infants' characteristics.
    Paper presented at the meeting of the American Psychological
    Association, Washington, D.C., 1982.

Ainsworth, M. D. S., Blehar, M. C., Waters, E., and Wall, S.
    Patterns of attachment. Hillsdale: Lawrence Erlbaum Asso-
    ciates, 1978.

Anderson, C. Attachment in daily separations: reconceptualizing
    day care and maternal employment issues. Child Develop-
    ment, 1980, 51, 242-245.

Anderson, C., Nagle, R., Roberts, W., and Smith, J. Attach-
    ment to substitute caregivers as a function of center quality
    and caregiver involvement. Child Development, 1981, 52,
    53-61.

Belsky, J. Future directions for day care research: an eco-
    logical analysis. Child Care Quarterly, 1980, 9, 82-99.

Belsky, J., and Steinberg, L. The effects of day care: a
    critical review. Child Development, 1978, 49, 929-949.

Blanchard, J., and Main, J. Avoidance of the attachment
    figure and social-emotional adjustment in day care infants.
    Developmental Psychology, 1979, 15, 445-446.

Blehar, M. Anxious Attachment and Defensive Reactions
    Associated with Day Care. Child Development, 1974, 45,
    683-692.

Bronfenbrenner, U. The ecology of human development. Cam-
    bridge: Harvard University Press, 1979.

Chibuco, T. R. and Chibuco, P. E. Adjustment of the Infant
    to Group Case: Quality of Parent-Infant Relationship. Paper
    presented at the Biennial Meeting of The Society for Research
    in Child Development. Detroit, Michigan, 1983.

Cohen, L. J. The operational definition of human attachment.
    Psychological Bulletin, 1974, 81, 207-217.

Cummings, E. M. The effect of stability of caregivers on social
    development in infant day care (Doctoral dissertation,
    University of California, Los Angeles, 1977). Dissertation
    Abstracts International, 1978, 38, 6005A-6006A. University
    Microfilms No. 7802598).

Cummings, E. M. Caregiver stability and day care. Develop-
    mental Psychology, 1980, 16, 31-37.

Farran, D. and Ramey, C. Infant day care and attachment
    behaviors toward mothers and teachers. Child Development,
    1977, 48, 1112-1116.

Fein, G. C. and Clarke-Stewart, A. Day care in context.
    New York: John Wiley & Sons, 1973.

Finkelstein, N. W. Aggression: Is it stimulated by day care?
    Young Children, September 1982.

Frye, D. The problem of infant day care. In E. F. Zigler and E. W. Gordon (Eds.), Day care: Scientific and social policy issues. Boston: Auburn, 1982.

Goldsmith, H. H. and Campos, J. J. Toward a theory of infant temperament. In R. N. Emde and R. J. Harmon (Eds.), The development of attachment and affiliative systems. New York: Plenum Press, 1982.

Hildebrand, J. Minding the kids. Newsday, September 26-29, 1982.

Hock, E. The transition to day care: Effects of maternal separation anxiety on infant adjustment, this volume.

Howes, C. and Rubenstein, J. Determinants of toddlers' experience in day care: Social-affective style, age of entry, and quality of setting. Unpublished manuscript, 1983.

Krentz, M. S. Qualitative differences between mother-child and caregiver-child attachments of infants in family day care. Paper presented at the biennial meeting of the Society for Research in Child Development. Detroit, Michigan, 1983.

Lamb, M. E. Interactions between eight month-old children and their fathers and mothers. In M. E. Lamb (Ed.), The role of the father in child development. New York, Wiley, 1976b.

Lamb, M. E. Interactions between two year-olds and their mothers and fathers. Psychological Research, 1976, 38, 447-450c.

Long, F., Garduque, L., and Peters, D. L. Continuity between home and family day care. Paper presented at the biennial meeting of the Society for Research in Child Development, Detroit, 1983.

Main, M., and Weston, D. R. The quality of the toddler's relationship to mother and to father: Related to conflict behavior and the readiness to establish new relationships. Child Development, 1981, 52, 932-940.

McCartney, K., Scarr, S., Phillips, D., Grajek, S., and
     Schwarz, C. Environmental differences among day care
     centers and their effects on children's development. In
     E. Zigler and E. W. Gordon (Eds.), Day Care. Boston,
     Auburn, 1982.

Moore, T. Exclusive early mothering and its alternatives:
     the outcome to adolescence. Scandanavian Journal of Psy-
     chology, 1975, 16, 255-272.

Moskowitz, D., Schwarz, J., and Corsini, D. Initiating day
     care at three years of age: effects on attachment. Child
     Development, 1977, 48, 1271-1276.

Pastor, D. L. The quality of mother-infant attachment and
     its relationship to toddlers' initial sociability with peers.
     Developmental Psychology, 1981, 17(3), 326-335.

Portnoy, F., and Simmons, C. Day Care and attachment.
     Child Development, 1978, 49, 239-242.

Prescott, E., Jones, E., Kritchevsky, S., Milich, C., and
     Haselhoef, E. Who thrives in group day care? Pasadena:
     Pacific Oaks College, 1975.

Provence, S. A program for group care for young children.
     Psychological Process, 1974, 3, 7-13.

Ricciuti, H. Fear and development of social attachments in
     the first year of life. In The Origins of Human Behavior:
     Fear. M. Lewis and L. Rosenblum (Eds.). New York:
     John Wiley & Sons, 1974.

Rubenstein, J. and Howes, C. Caregiving and infant behavior
     in day care and in homes. Developmental Psychology, 1979,
     17, 113-120.

Rubenstein, J., Pedersen, F., and Yarrow, L. What happens
     when mother is away: a comparison of mothers and substitute
     caregivers. Developmental Psychology, 1977, 13, 529-530.

Rutter, M. Social-emotional consequences of day care for pre-
     school children. American Journal of Orthopsychiatry,
     1981, 51, 4-28.

Schwartz, P. Length of day care attendance and attachment behavior in eighteen-month old infants. Child Development, 1983, 54, 1073-1078.

Schwarz, J., Krolick, G., and Strickland, R. Effects of early day care experience on adjustment to a new environment. American Journal of Orthopsychiatry, 1973, 43, 340-346.

Schwarz, J., Strickland, R., and Krolick, G. Infant day care: behavioral effects at preschool age. Developmental Psychology, 1974, 10, 502-506.

Strayer, F. F. Social ecology of the preschool peer group. In W. A. Collins (Ed.). The Minnesota symposia on child psychology, Vol. 13. Hillsdale, N.J.: Lawrence Erlbaum Associates, 1980.

Strayer, F. F. The organization and coordination of asymmetrical relations among young children: A biological view of social power. In M. D. Watts (Ed.). New Directions for Methodology of Social and Behavioral Science, 7, 1981.

Strayer, F. F. and Noel, J. M. Triadic conflict among young children: An ethological study of prosocial and antisocial aggression. In Zahn-Waxler, C., Cummings, E. M., and Radke-Yarrow, M. Altruism and aggression: Social and biological origins, in press.

Travers, J. and Ruopp, R. National Day Care Study: Preliminary Findings and Their Implications. Cambridge, MA: ABT Associates, Inc., 1978.

Vaughn, B. E., Gove, F. L., and Egeland, B. The relationship between out-of-home care and quality of infant-mother attachment in an economically disadvantaged population. Child Development, 1980, 51, 1203-1214.

Waters, E., Wippman, J., and Sroufe, L. A. Attachment, positive affect, and competence in the peer group: Two studies in construct validation. Child Development, 1979, 50, 821-829.

Wilcox, B., Staff, P., and Romaine, M. A comparison of individual and multiple assignment of caregivers to infants in day care. Merrill-Palmer Quarterly, 1980, 26, 53-62.

Zaslow, M., Rabinovich, B., Suwalsky, J. Impact on the
    Child of Maternal Employment: An Examination of Mediating
    Variables. In E. S. Collin (Ed.), Developmental Plasticity:
    Social Context and Human Development. Academic Press
    (in press).

The Transition to Day Care:
Effects of Maternal Separation Anxiety
on Infant Adjustment

Ellen Hock

INTRODUCTION

In order to fully comprehend the child's adaptation to day care, Bronfenbrenner (1979) has suggested that we must look beyond the immediate day care context and examine the transition between the familiar home setting and the new day care setting. Perhaps it would be wise to identify a unique area for study which would be labelled the study of the separation setting. Study of the separation setting would involve examination of the physical surroundings and the emotions and interpersonal actions which occur in the transition period when a parent leaves an infant at a day care center or any instance in which a parent temporarily transfers the care of and responsibility for the infant to a caregiver.

Much attention has been given to the study of parent-infant interaction in the home setting and caregiver-infant interaction in the day care setting. It is somewhat surprising, though, that researchers have given so little attention to the study of the separation event because for parents, teachers, and certainly for infants, the separation is a terribly significant event—often dreaded, often traumatic and, at the least, predictably worrisome.

Importance of the Separation Setting

While there is little doubt that the concerns of parents, caregivers, and infants are a valid motive for pursuing a study

of the separation event, there are other significant conceptual
and theoretical problems that are addressed by focusing on
the separation event. One primary concern for developmental
psychologists is the long term consequences of an early event.
One naturally tends to pose the question: If the first separations
of parent and infant are successfully negotiated, will later
separations of the child and significant others be more easily
handled? It is reasonable to suggest that if the early parent-
infant separations are not too difficult and result in an overall
positive experience, then the child's experience in the absence
of the parent will tend to be more positive and future separations
less fear-provoking and difficult. Conversely, if the early
separation goes badly and intense negative emotions are associated with the separation event, the child will be apprehensive
about future separations and will dread experiencing those
negative emotions as well; in other words, he will fear the
experiencing of fearful feelings and the anxieties associated
with the separation event will not diminish; rather than subsequent separations becoming easier, the anticipation of fear will
compound the problems. The parent will react to the child's
distress and the anxiety of both will escalate.

It is important to expand these considerations and to merge
them into the flow of human development beyond infants; that
is, we need to go beyond the immediate concerns of parent-
infant day care separation in order to accentuate the relevance
of early experiences with separation to experience over the life
span. Michael Rutter, in his major address to the Society for
Research in Child Development in 1983, discussed the mechanism
of continuity; that is, the mechanism whereby early events
influence later development. Of particular relevance to our
concern with early separation events, he discussed the concept
of "sensitization effects." In this context he provided the
example associated with parent-infant separations, stating that
if the earlier separations were handled well and resulted in a
"happy separation," future separations would lead to more
adaptive responses. There are meaningful links over the
course of time and one such link is nested in the concept that
successful separations will lead to adaptive responses which
will lead to future successful separations over the course of
the child's life.

It is clear that there are important reasons to direct our
investigative efforts to the better understanding of the separation event. As the examples previously discussed have illus-
trated, study of the separation event must involve a consideration
of how the infant responds to separation as well as how the

parent's feelings about separation influence the infant. The
infant's response to separation has been well studied and will
be considered here only briefly. The unique contribution of
the chapter will be its focus on parental, primarily maternal,
concerns about separation, particularly the way in which
parental anxiety about separation can be measured and how
the infant's adaptation to separation can be influenced by the
parent's anxiety.

In the early 1970s there was ample documentation about
the occurrence of infant separation protest and separation
anxiety in infants. Studies by Schaffer (1977), Ainsworth
(1963), Yarrow (1967) and theoretical contributions of Bowlby
(1973) provided understanding of the infant's response to
separation from the mother. Yet, no mention had been made
about how mothers or fathers felt about separation. Schaffer
(1977) stated,

> Research on the effects of separation provides
> a vivid indication of the strong emotional forces
> that bind the child to his mother. It is a pity,
> however, that no comparable studies have illus-
> trated the effects on the mother. The almost
> exclusive attention on the child may suggest, if
> not that the mother is unaffected by the experi-
> ence, at least that she is left unchanged by it.
> Yet Robert Hinde has shown that in rhesus
> monkeys the post-separation disturbance found
> in infants is caused primarily by the distortions
> separation brings about in the mother's behavior.
> The animals' capacity for precisely synchronized
> interaction breaks down during the separation
> period, so that for a while after reunion the
> mothers are unable to continue the relationship
> quite as before. It is highly unlikely that similar
> clear-cut effects can be found in human mothers.
> Nevertheless, the animal data underline the fact
> that it is the couple that has become separated
> and not just the child, and that both individuals
> rather than just one must subsequently readjust.
> (Schaffer, 1977, p. 97-98)

THE SEPARATION SETTING: MATERNAL BEHAVIOR

To date, child development researchers have focused
almost exclusively on the infant's behavior during separation.

However, a few studies have examined infants' responses to selected maternal behaviors exhibited before or during a leavetaking. (It is important to note that in these studies maternal behavior is studied, not maternal attitudes or emotions.) Four studies have examined the impact of maternal leavetaking behavior on the child's response to specific behaviors exhibited by the parent as he/she left the child. Specifically, Weinraub and Lewis (1977) noted verbal and nonverbal behavior of both mothers and children during free play, departure, and separation situations. These observations yielded three maternal departure styles which varied with respect to the amount and type of information mothers gave their children regarding their departure. One group left without any mention to the child of their departure. A second group of mothers informed the children that they were leaving and would return. Finally, a third group told the children of their departure and/or return and also told them what to do during the separation. Maternal departure style was found to have a direct effect on the child's separation distress, defined in terms of the amount of time the child spent playing during separation episodes. Mothers who provided their child with information regarding their departure had children who evidenced the least separation distress.

In order to differentiate between the amount of information given to the child at leavetaking and the time taken to relay the information, Adams and Passman (1981) exposed two-year olds to brief and extended departures. In the brief departure situation, mothers were asked to make ten second statements informing their child they they would return soon and that the child should play. In the extended departure, mothers were asked to spend 40 seconds using various statements informing the child about the separation. In both conditions, similar information was provided to the children and the amount of verbal interaction was controlled because mothers in the brief departure condition were asked to say nursery rhymes as fillers before delivering departure messages. By manipulating maternal departure style, they found that children of mothers who gave brief (ten second) explanations regarding separation played longer and with more toys during the mother's absence than did children whose mothers provided longer, somewhat repetitive explanations. That an extended explanation proves less beneficial to parental-child separation than a brief explanation suggests that parental behavior during separation can markedly affect child behavior. This can be seen more clearly in a more recent study.

   In another study examining parental behavior and separation distress in infants, Weinraub and Frankel (1977) observed
naturally-occuring separation behavior of parents of 18-month
old children. Parents were asked to engage in a fifteen-minute
free-play session and to depart in any way that they felt comfortable. Parent and infant behaviors were scored as they had
been in Weinraub and Lewis (1977). The results indicated that
fathers made more verbal statements to the children than did
mothers. Infants who were left by a same-sex parent were
less distressed upon separation than those leaving opposite-sex
parents. Effects of sex of child and sex of parent were found
for the amount of information given to the infant on departure.
That is, more information given girls by their mothers upon
departure was significantly correlated with less play (more
distress) during the mother's absence. This relationship was
not found for fathers leaving their daughters, or for either
parent leaving a son.

   Field et al. (1983) examined leavetaking and reunion
behaviors of infants, toddlers, and preschoolers enrolled in
preschool, and their parents, in order to identify optimal
departure/reunion styles for child-parent dyads. Daily observations of leavetaking and greeting occurred in two six-week
intervals which were six months apart. Behavior of both parents
and children were observed from arrival and departure using
behavior checklists designed to reflect behaviors characteristically observed. Then 15 leavetakings were randomly selected
from each six-week period for analysis. Age and sex differences
in arrival behavior were found; infants and toddlers interacted
mostly with parents while preschoolers spent more time with
teachers. Girls were more likely to interact with teachers,
whereas boys were more likely to approach the children's play
activities. Regarding the separation of parent and child,
toddlers showed the most distress at parental departure.
Parents of toddlers more often hovered about the children
and "sneaked out of the room" than parents of older and younger
children. When mothers versus fathers dropped off children,
more attention-getting behavior and crying occurred. However,
mothers engaged in more behavior designed to distract the
child and showed a longer latency to leave the classroom than
fathers. In the second six-week period of observation, it was
noted that parent-child dyads spent less time interacting at
leavetaking, fewer protestations occurred at separation, and
parents left the classroom more quickly. A number of parent-
behaviors appeared to relate to child distress at leavetaking:

verbal explanation, distracting the child, latency to leave, and "sneaking out of the room." Leavetaking distress was also related to children's ambivalence at reunion.

Taken together, these studies suggest a strong linkage between parent behavior during separation and infant behavior. It is surprising in view of the consistency of these findings that maternal attitudes about separation and anxiety in separation settings has not been systematically examined.

MATERNAL ATTITUDES AND EMOTIONS SURROUNDING SEPARATION

While these studies provide interesting findings regarding the child's response to specific parental behaviors related to separation, parental concerns or anxiety about separation from their infants and the transmission of this anxiety to the child remains largely an unexplored area. A number of investigators have recognized the importance of maternal attitude and feelings towards separation (e.g., Field et al., 1983; Weinraub and Lewis, 1977; Weinraub and Frankel, 1977). In particular, Field et al. (1983), alluded to the role of maternal anxiety in stating "Parents may behave in ways which are consistent with their worries and expectations and their behaviors may reinforce their child's behaviors" (p. 10). In addition, Weinraub and Lewis (1977) describe the relationship between types of mother-child interaction and maternal emotional states. They describe three major aspects of mother-child free-play interaction including mother-child proximity accompanied by little child play, mother-child proximity with shared play activity, and distal interaction which included the child and mother looking at or talking with one another. The types of interaction were related to separation distress in the infant. Children who engaged in close, shared activity and touching with mothers were more likely to be distressed in their absence. Weinraub and Lewis (1977) concluded that the mother seems to serve as cue for the child's behavior and "The emotional quality of the mother-child relationship (i.e., the quality of the mother-child attachment) may influence [sic] on separation distress by affecting the amount of interaction preseparation" (p. 57). When Weinraub and Lewis (1977) considered social class differences, it was suggested that some mothers may feel more uncomfortable than others when observed in unnatural situations and this uneasiness may be communicated to their children. They suggest that in much previous research, the mother's spontaneous behavior in a separation incident is suppressed, resulting in the mother's

unusual behavior. Thus the mother's unnatural behavior may
be perceived by the infant.

Weinraub and Frankel (1977) asked parents to predict
how they thought their child would respond in a subsequent
laboratory sequence in order to assess parental anticipation
of separation. Parents were interviewed following the laboratory
separation situation and asked how they felt during their child's
absence. The majority of mothers expected their 18-month old
children to cry when they left while only about one-third of the
fathers predicted that their child would cry. Slightly less than
half of the mothers said that they worried about their infants
response to their absence while none of the fathers reported
being worried. Unfortunately, these responses were not
related to infants' actual degree of distress at separation in
the study. However, the results suggest that maternal negative
responses to separation exceeded paternal concerns. There
are, of course, questions about how the mother's emotional
state is transmitted to the infant and how sensitive infants are
to changes in their mother's affective tone.

Infant Perception of Maternal Emotions

Two recent studies (Cohn, 1981; Sorce, Emde, and Klinnert, 1981) provide support for the notion that the mother's
emotional state does affect the infant. Cohn (1981), studied
24 three-month old infants' responses to the affective quality
of their mothers' behavior. Cohn manipulated the affective
quality of maternal behavior: he trained mothers, by using
verbal instruction and videotape, to simulate maternal depression.
The effect was to slow down the pace of interaction, eliminate
smiles and bright faces, and to limit body movement. When
mothers in the depressed condition interacted with their babies,
the major proportion of the infants' time was spent on behaviors
labelled "wary," "protest," and "look away." The depressed
condition proved quite stressful with one quarter of the infants
crying steadily for 30 seconds or more. Even more striking was
the finding that infants who were exposed to the depressed
condition remained significantly more wary during the first
minute of subsequent normal interaction than those from the
non-depressed condition. Cohn noted,

> These results strongly support our hypothesis that
> infants are able to regulate their own behavior in
> response to their mother's affective displays.
> Infant behavior in response to normal interaction

tends to be well organized and to cycle predomi-
nantly among neutral and positive states. When
mothers act depressed their infants respond by
attempting to elicit a change in the mother's affect
and failing that, their behavior becomes negative
and less well organized. The infants become relα-
tively absorbed in a negative cycle, and these
differences are likely to carry into the next period
of normal interaction (Cohn, 1981, p. 6-7).

Particularly relevant to the study of the transmission of
maternal anxiety to the infant is the work of Sorce et al. (1981)
who examined the infant's ability to "read" maternal emotional
tones. They hypothesized that, when faced with a situation
which arouses cognitive-affective uncertainty, the child may
use the mother's emotional responses to the situation in determining his/her own response. They suggested that positively
toned maternal emotional signals (e.g., interest and enjoyment)
may encourage approach, exploratory, or playful activity in
the infant, while negatively toned emotions (e.g., fear and
anger) on the part of the mother may result in retreat or
avoidance behaviors in the infant.

The researchers watched 36 one-year old infants in a
visual cliff situation and systematically varied the facial expression of the mother who sat within view of the infant. Results
revealed a dramatic effect of mother's emotional signaling on
infant behaviors. When mother posed a fearful expression
none of the infants ventured across the deep side. In contrast,
14 or the 19 infants who observed mother's smiling face did
cross the deep side. "These results clearly indicate that one-
year old infants do make use of mother's emotional signal to
guide their behaviors in times of uncertainty or mild apprehension. These emotional signals were potent communicators even
though they were limited to the facial expression channel,
devoid of any vocal, postural, or gestural cues" (Sorce et al.,
1981, p. 9).

These studies clearly document that when the mother's
emotional tone is changed to reflect depression or fear, the
infant's behavior is affected accordingly. Other classic work
with older children in the areas of school phobia, dental fears,
and reaction to hospitalization also provides evidence to support
the view that maternal anxiety can be transmitted to the child.
Gerald Winer (1982), in a review of children's dental fears,
noted the importance of the correlation between maternal anxiety
and the child's negative behavior. Concerning the communication
of anxiety between parents and the children, Winer noted,

"There is some evidence suggesting that parental ploys designed
to ameliorate anxiety are, in fact, associated with increased
dental fears (e.g., Bailey et al., 1973; Otto, 1974). Thus,
when parents are attempting to calm children, they might, in
fact, be having precisely the opposite effect. This conclusion
receives support from research investigating reactions to
separation (Adams and Passman, 1981). Besides suggesting
subtle ways of communicating anxiety, the results imply that
children are adept at reading signals portending anxiety or
fear-provoking situations. It would be fascinating to manipulate
more specifically the communication between parents and children
in well-designed experimental studies" (Winer, 1982, p. 1130).

The school phobia literature provides a fascinating base
of support for the understanding of interactive dynamics
surrounding mother-child separation. The classic writings of
Eisenberg (1958) and Berecz (1968) and Waldron et al. (1975)
all discuss extensively the typical picture of the mother of the
school-phobic child, a mother who transmits her own ambivalence
about separation and her anxiety to the child. Waldfogel (1959)
wrote, "Like all phobias, the symptom in school phobia represents a displacement of anxiety" (Waldfogel et al., 1959, p. 756).
When the anxiety is traced to its source it is invariably found
to originate in the child's fear of being separated from his
mother. The child's anxiety about separation is an outgrowth
of the mother's own anxiety on this score. Davidson (1960)
observed, "It first appears that the mother is trying to persuade
the child to attend and that the child is refusing to go, but
later we see that the mother unconsciously prevents the child
from returning" (p. 205).

As these studies clearly document, the emotional state of
the mother is transmitted to the infant or young child. When
the mother's emotional tone is one of depression, anxiety, or
fear the infant's response is negative, one of withdrawal,
fretfulness, or clear distress.

The Study of Maternal Emotions
About Separation

In 1973, Hock designed a study to assess the effects of
several types of non-maternal care on the mother-infant relationship. Because, in 1973 when the data for this study were
collected, leaving an infant to return to work was not the norm
for mothers, it seemed relevant to ask the mothers participating
in the study how they felt about leaving their babies. Interview-
based measures of maternal concerns about separation from

their infants were added to other more extensive observational and interview-based assessments of mothers' personality, sensitivity of mothering behavior, and her attitudes about her own needs for self-fulfillment--e.g., needs related to pursuing a career.

The measures of mother's concerns about separation proved to be very interesting and were related to other maternal characteristics and to certain infant measures. Data from interviews and observations of the mothers at infant ages three and eight months were factor analyzed. The separation-related measures loaded on a factor labelled maternal separation anxiety; the separation anxiety factor was unrelated to the several other factors that seemed to reflect more traditional measures of sensitive, responsive caregiving. The factor analysis thus produced evidence in support of the idea that maternal emotions about separation as it was measured in this study was not simply another measure reflecting sensitivity or responsitivity to infant needs. It instead represented another dimension, a unique maternal attribute not systematically related to other measures.

This study, begun in 1973, was a longitudinal investigation. The infants and their mothers were seen in a lab observational setting when the infants were one year of age. One hundred sixty-four dyads participated. Infants' responses to separation were assessed with Ainsworth's Strange Situation Behavior Instrument (SSBI) (Ainsworth and Wittig, 1969). Hock (1976) reported that the measure of the mother's separation anxiety, as assessed in a home interview with the mother at eight months infant age, was related to infant behavior in the lab separation sequence (for this analysis, only the post-separation episode of the SSBI was used). A high level of maternal anxiety, as conveyed in the interview, was significantly correlated with high levels of infant contact-maintaining to mother (e.g., clinging), infant proximity seeking to mother, and crying.

In a subsequent study, Hock and Clinger (1981) explored infant coping behavior during separation from mother. Lois Murphy's (1962, 1976) view of coping behavior was adopted in the study; that is, coping is viewed as a process through which the individual comes to terms with a challenge or makes use of an opportunity. Murphy writes that the "drive toward mastery" underlies coping efforts and is expressed in them. Coping patterns are most easily seen when an individual is confronted with a new situation which cannot be handled by reflex, habit, or other routine or automatic action. Coping is the person's dealing with the actual external or objective situation; it may, but does not necessarily include defense mechanisms (Murphy, 1970).

The purpose of the Hock and Clinger (1981) coping study
was to describe and quantify coping behaviors of one-year olds
in relation to their abilities to befriend and/or use the resources
of an unfamiliar female adult to allay the stress of maternal
separation in an unfamiliar environment. Moreover, relationships
of maternal attitudes about separation to the infant's coping
behaviors were studied. In this analysis of strange situation
data, a system for categorizing babies according to their abilities
to cope with the stresses of the mother's absence was developed.
In addition, only those episodes of the SSBI in which the
stranger was present were utilized (episodes 3, 4, and 7).
Five characteristic patterns of coping were observed which
differed primarily in the degree to which the infant made use
of non-maternal resources:

(a) Resource rejecting: The infant is extremely wary of
the stranger and in the mother's absence is greatly distressed
and is unable to relate to the stranger and/or the environment.
(b) Resource resisting: The infant is wary of the stranger
and in the mother's absence is distressed and is unable to
relate to the stranger, but is able to indicate desire for
the mother by repeatedly looking, pointing, or going to the
door.
(c) Passive observer: The infant is passive and shows little
or no reaction to the events and/or persons in the immediate
environment.
(d) Resource accepting: The infant interacts with the
stranger but only after the stranger has initiated it; in the
mother's absence the infant may become somewhat distressed
but is able to relate to the stranger and/or environment as
a source of comfort.
(e) Positive affect/initiating: The infant is affectively
positive and outgoing, and initiates interaction with the
stranger. In the mother's absence the infant does not
become distressed and continues to interact with the stranger
and/or goes to the door and tries to open it (Hock and
Clinger, 1981).

The findings demonstrated that maternal attitudes about
separation (assessed when the infants were eight months old)
were significantly related to infant coping. Infants of mothers
who perceived themselves as being irreplaceable (i.e., they
believed that their babies would be greatly distressed during
separation and that only the mother could meet her baby's needs)

were most distressed and least likely to be coded as resource accepting.

These early studies were not originally designed to examine the effects of maternal separation anxiety; in fact, assessments of mothers' feelings about separation represented a comparatively small part of the data collected. However, the findings from these analyses suggested the following important ideas: 1) maternal attitudes and emotions about separation represent a unique dimension of the maternal personality, distinct from traditional "quality of mothering" measures and 2) interview-based measures of maternal separation anxiety obtained before the infants were nine months old were related to infant behavior observed during mother-infant separation in the laboratory when the infants were twelve months old. In sum, the way a mother feels about separation could be measured and this measure represented something different from other traditional measures of maternal attributes; in addition, there was reason to believe that the way the mother felt about separation influenced infant adaptation to separation. Certainly further study of maternal feelings about separation was warranted. In 1981, Hock initiated a series of studies aimed at defining and measuring maternal separation anxiety.

Developing a Measure of Maternal
Separation Anxiety

A working definition of maternal separation anxiety was generated in order to guide the development of assessment techniques. Maternal separation anxiety is an unpleasant emotional state reflecting a mother's apprehension about leaving her child. A mother's expressions describing feelings of sadness, worry, or uneasiness about being away from her child indicate a transitory state of anxiety which is uniquely associated with separation events. In addition to verbal expressions, maternal separation anxiety may be reflected in behaviors mothers exhibit before they leave the child, during their departure, and upon reunion with the child.

Consideration was given to four factors that underlie a mother's expression of concern about separating from her child. The assumption was that the anxiety a mother experienced on leaving a child is influenced by 1) her own personality attributes (e.g., nurturance and dependence) that lead to feelings of depression and fear about separation and loss. As an outgrowth of her own needs, separation from her child may be a

stressful situation causing expressions of worry and concern.
Guilt at leaving the child may be a pervasive emotion; 2) the
mother's conviction that mothers are uniquely capable of caring
for their child, i.e., she believes that only a mother can really
satisfy a child's needs and therefore any option other than
exclusive maternal care elicits guilt and anxiety; 3) the mother's
perceptions of the child's ability to adapt; her degree of conviction that the child can adjust to and benefit from care provided
by others. She will be more anxious if she believes that the
child will not adapt well to nonmaternal care; and 4) her belief,
of socio-cultural origin, about women's roles—particularly with
respect to the balance between motherhood and a career or job
that would necessitate mother/child separation. This dimension
reflects her degree of investment in the traditional conception
of the maternal role versus her desire to pursue a career or
job outside the home. If she is highly invested in a traditional
concept of the maternal role she will be more anxious about job-
related mother-child separation.

   Thus, a mother's concern about separation may stem from
multiple sources, ranging from her concern about the child's
ability to adapt to nonmaternal care to her own role-related
conflicts. In developing a questionnaire, these four sources
of anxiety needed to be tapped to effectively measure a mother's
overall level of concern about separation. Items for the self-
administered questionnaire were generated so that each of these
four areas of concern were represented by several questions.*

   A 68-item scale was developed and, in order to explore
its psychometric properties, was administered to a large sample
of women who were mothers of firstborn infants. All women
who had delivered full-term healthy babies between October
1981 and January 1982 in three large metropolitan hospitals
were contacted. Demographic information was obtained and the
68-item separation anxiety scale was administered along with
the Taylor Manifest Anxiety Scale and the Edwards Social
Desirability Scale. Complete data was obtained from 620 women
(Hock, Gnezda, and McBride, 1983).

   Interestingly, the separation anxiety scale scores were
moderately correlated with the manifest anxiety scale scores

---

   *Several individuals working together in 1981 at the Ohio
State University generated the items for the first 68-item version
of the Maternal Separation Anxiety Scale. Ellen Hock and three
doctoral students, M. Therese Gnezda, Susan McBride, and
Ellen Martin-Huff participated in this initial work.

($\underline{r}$ = .34, $\underline{p}$ < .05). This finding reflected an expected (and conceptually ideal) relationship; increased "trait" anxiety was predictive of increased maternal separation anxiety, but the magnitude of the coefficient suggests that trait anxiety does not fully account for all the variation in separation anxiety. The degree of relationship between the separation anxiety scores and the social desirability scale scores was also appropriate ($\underline{r}$ = -.39, $\underline{p}$ < .05); scales assessing social desirability should relate negatively to scales measuring neuroticism and anxiety (Nunally, 1978).

In order to fully explore the psychometric properties of the newly developed separation anxiety scale, an exploratory principal component factor analysis was performed. A three-factor model provided the best fit for the data (Hock, Gnezda, and McBride, 1983).

The first factor, labelled "Maternal Separation Anxiety" was loaded on by items generated to tap the 1st and 2nd hypothesized sources of anxiety described above; that is, questions directly inquiring about the levels of maternal guilt and sadness and questions focusing on beliefs about a mother's unique ability to care for a child composed Factor 1. Examples of such items are:

●When I am away from my child, I feel lonely and miss/him her a great deal.
●I don't enjoy myself when I'm away from my child.

Factor II was defined as "Separation Promotes Independence" and corresponds to dimension three, a mother's beliefs about her child's ability to adapt to and profit from nonmaternal care. Sample items are:

●Exposure to many different people is good for my child.
●My child needs to spend time away from me in order to develop a sense of being an individual in his/her own right.

The third factor corresponded to the fourth dimension which addressed the balance between maternal role and employment and was subsequently labelled "Employment-Related Separation Concerns." Examples of item loading on this factor included:

●I would resent my job if it meant I had to be away from my child.
●I would not regret postponing my career in order to stay home with my child.

In order to investigate the temporal stability of the scale, it was readministered to the mother three months after the initial administration. The time$_1$, time$_2$ correlation was .78 indicating an acceptable level of over-time consistency.

Inspection of findings produced by factor analysis and item analysis led to the conclusion that the test could be strengthened by reducing the number of items to 35. Strong items representing each of the 3 factors were selected; the final version of the questionnaire consisted of 21 items representing Factor 1, 7 items representing Factor 2 and 7 items representing Factor 3.

Regarding the internal consistency of the 35-item scale, the Cronbach's coefficient alpha for the 21 items composing Factor I, Maternal Separation Anxiety, was .90. The reliability coefficient for Factor II, Separation Promotes Independence was .77, and the coefficient alpha for Factor III, Employment-Related Separation Concerns, was .71. The internal consistency of the total 35-item MSAS was .89 (Hock, Gnezda, and McBride, 1983).

In summary, the 35-item Maternal Separation Anxiety Scale (MSAS) is characterized by strong internal consistency and good over-time (test-retest) reliability. The items are relevant to separation from children from birth through kindergarten age and the wording is easily understood by adults of all educational levels. With minor changes the items can be adapted to be administered to either mothers or fathers. (However, the Factor 3 items about career versus homemaking are not really meaningful for fathers--role-related conflicts stemming from socio-cultural sex role proscriptions are probably not as severe a source of conflict for fathers.)

A recent study (Martin-Huff, 1982) examined the relationship between parents' separation anxiety scores and the adjustment of their children to kindergarten. The children who were recruited represented the entire kindergarten population of four elementary schools in two suburban school districts who were from two-parent families and were entering for the first time into formal public schooling. The Maternal Separation Anxiety Scale (labelled "Attitudes About Childcare" for purposes of this study) was mailed to both parents of the 135 children prior to the first day of school. The First Grade Adjustment Scale (Medinnus, 1961) was used by the classroom teachers to rate the children's adjustment to kindergarten. The items on this scale are grouped into five subscales: Physical Status and Motor Behavior, Social Behavior, Emotional Behavior, Intellectual Abilities and Behavior, and Adjustment to Classroom Membership and Requirements. The classroom teachers rated each child two times: once after the second week of school and again following the sixth week of school.

Interestingly, the fathers as a group scored similarly to mothers on the first two factors of the separation anxiety scale. As expected, on Factor III, Employment-Related Separation Concerns, fathers' responses reflected much less anxiety. It would appear that traditional sex-role proscriptions do not function to engender anxiety and guilt when fathers leave their children to pursue their jobs/careers.

Analysis of the relationship between maternal separation anxiety (Factor I on the Maternal Separation Anxiety Scale) and five child adjustment scale scores produced a consistent pattern of findings. The greater the mothers' separation anxiety, the lower the child's adjustment. Specifically, maternal separation anxiety assessed by Factor I was significantly, negatively related to Physical State and Motor Behavior, Emotional Behavior, Intellectual Abilities, Adjustment to Classroom, and the Total Adjustment Score.

These findings are important because they clearly demonstrate that the child's adjustment is related to the mother's separation anxiety. Of course, the dynamics underlying that relationship are unclear. We might ask if there is a causal relationship wherein mother's anxiety is transmitted to the child; perhaps in very subtle ways the mother's uneasiness gives the child the message that there is something to be feared in the school experience. That, somehow, if mother is not comfortable about his going to school then indeed, there is something about this new setting that is not to be trusted. This line of reasoning is certainly plausible and provocative but there are other alternative explanations for the maternal anxiety-child adjustment relationship and the problem is complex. The culture, the family system, and the child's characteristics certainly contribute to the relationship. To fully understand how maternal anxiety affects infants and young children we must recognize the complexity of this network of interacting influences.

IMPLICATIONS FOR PARENTS
AND CAREGIVERS

Individual differences in children's responses and adjustment to day care have been repeatedly documented in the research literature and typically accounted for in terms of day care setting characteristics, e.g., the quantitative and qualitative aspects of the caregiver-child interaction. A less frequently explored factor suggested by the current review is maternal attitudes regarding separation. As noted above, young children have been shown to be highly sensitive to maternal affect, including her anxiety in anticipation of separation and her response to mother-child separation.

These findings, while suggesting the need for further research in the area of maternal separation anxiety, also have implications regarding day care practice and policy. In this section, several direct implications for mothers and caregivers will be described. Acknowledgment of maternal anxiety which can be evoked by the day care situation is important and counseling mothers about their feelings could be useful. As well, optimal leavetaking strategies have been suggested in the research literature as facilitators of positive separations. A number of more indirect means of reducing or minimizing maternal separation anxiety will be suggested including parental understanding of infant separation protest, monitoring characteristics of the home and day care routine for the infant, and the degree to which the day care setting fits maternal needs.

The research reviewed in this chapter strongly indicates the need for professionals and parents to acknowledge separation anxiety and to better understand the cause of these feelings. Research indicating marked impact of maternal behavior and attitudes on infant behavior at separation and subsequent infant participation in day care activities suggests that dealing with maternal separation anxiety and taking steps toward its reduction can contribute to positive day care adjustment for both mother and child. Mothers need to understand that feelings of separation anxiety are experienced by many women who have both a career or job and a family. Acknowledging that they have fears and worries related to leaving the child with a caregiver is important.

Suggestions for maternal/parental leavetaking styles can be drawn from the research findings presented. Ultimately, parents will develop strategies which suit the individual needs of their child, but certain maternal behaviors have been associated with positive reactions to separation and these could be incorporated into departure repertoires. Providing some information about the departure seems to facilitate infant adjustment after maternal separation (Weinraub and Lewis, 1977). A simple, "I'm leaving now" may be all that is needed to convey that it is time to leave, allowing the infant to make the transition. Perhaps it may be beneficial for the mother to signal departure time in this way because she has initiated the transition herself rather than leaving the caretaker to explain her absence to the child. Research has also shown that this transmission of information is better brief than extended (Adams and Passman, 1981; Field et al., 1983). In addition to associations with reduced infant distress at departure, Cummings and Beagles-Ross (this volume) suggested that mothers who took longer to complete the separation, particularly with boys, may be more reluctant to leave or have more anxiety than fathers who had much briefer separation sequences. Getting in the habit of making a short leavetaking may reduce the infant's distress and indirectly may serve to reduce maternal anxiety. Rositer (1982) sums up these recommendations in the following way:

> A short, clear goodbye routine gives the child the
> message that the parent is leaving and that every-
> thing is alright. If the baby holds on or cries, he
> can be given to the caregiver and the usual routine
> continued. As long as the parent follows through
> with the departure without ambivalently prolonging
> the moment, the child will more readily accept the
> situation and return to relaxed play (Rositer, 1982,
> p. 9).

Apart from maternal behaviors which can promote positive separation and thus minimize separation anxiety, there are a number of strategies which should be avoided. The findings of Field et al. (1983) suggest that hovering about the child, trying to distract the child from maternal leavetaking, or leaving without the child's knowledge do not promote positive separations. If possible, mothers should stay calm about infant protest at leavetaking; clinging and crying should be received with comfort and assurance (Rodriguez and Hignett, 1981).

These recommendations illustrate an important gap in the research literature: Our knowledge of optimal separation strategies with respect to reducing the mother's ambivalence or reluctance at separation and consequent anxiety is based on common sense or confined to speculation. We know very little about how to help a mother pace the leavetaking so that both she and the infant will be comfortable. Perhaps there are minor changes in routines and common practices that could be implemented, e.g., mothers might be reassured if they could routinely check back through a one-way mirror after leaving their infant.

Perhaps examining the ways in which infant distress can be minimized will suggest indirect ways to reduce maternal anxiety or confirm those we have already recommended. An

approach to easing separation distress and maternal anxiety is
to monitor aspects of the infant's home and day care environment which could exacerbate difficult separations. Rodriguez
and Hignett (1981) recommend that aspects of the physical
environment not be altered during developmental periods of
intense separation distress. Rodriguez and Hignett (1981)
also suggest that continuity in caregivers be maintained. They
write:

> . . . The introduction of "strange" adults such as
> students, volunteers, and substitutes should be
> kept to a minimum. Other unnecessary changes
> at the center should also be avoided. Critical
> among these shifts in the environment is the care-
> giver herself. Unfortunately, it is often accepted
> policy to "promote" the infants at twelve months
> to another caregiver or room. Alternatives to this
> common policy should be sought. (p. 9)

This suggestion is supported by the research of Cummings
and Beagles-Ross (this volume) who noted that continuity of
caregivers contributed to more positive emotional functioning,
less separation distress, and more positive affect following
separation. Small group size was also associated with better
child separations.

Thus, in addition to establishing routines of separation,
aspects of the separation setting may reduce maternal anxiety.
Further suggestions for promoting optimum separations can be
made by considering the nature of the substitute care.

The mother's choice of and adjustment to the day care
setting is important in minimizing maternal anxiety. With the
focus on the mother, the overriding consideration becomes that
of helping her to feel comfortable with the day care arrangements.
For example, facilitating trust in the substitute caretaker may
help to minimize maternal anxiety. Rositer points out how
easily poor parent-caregiver relations can evolve.

> Because the set of expectations and style of care
> each adult uses with a baby can vary widely, day
> care is ripe with opportunities for conflict. Also,
> with children under six months of age, parental
> feelings of jealousy and anger are most intense,
> especially for a first-time parent taking the baby
> to an experienced caregiver. Recognizing the
> potential for problems and openly discussing them

with the day care staff are the first steps toward
their resolution. There is a point where parents
can learn from the caregiver; there is also a point
where the parents must assert their judgment and
desires—even if they are seen as 'wrong' by the
day care staff (Rositer, 1982, p. 3-4).

These types of stresses associated with jealousy or conflict
with the caregiver could certainly contribute to maternal anxiety.
    That some mothers will continue to have serious misgivings
about day care in spite of implementation of the above recommendations is inevitable. Employers need to make available
viable alternatives for working women such as extended maternity
leave, paternity leave, and on-site day care. Given the growing
number of women in the work force today and the evidence
which suggests that the mother's adjustment to day care impacts
on the child's adjustment, implementation of such policies is
warranted.

REFERENCES

Adams, R. E., and Passman, R. H. The effects of preparing
    two-year olds for brief separations from their mothers.
    Child Development, 1981, 52, 1068-1070.

Ainsworth, M. D. The development of infant-mother interaction
    among the Ganda. In B. M. Foss (Ed.), Determinants of
    infant behavior II. London: Metheum, 1963.

Ainsworth, M. D. and Wittig, B. A. Attachment and explora-
    tory behavior in one-year olds in a strange situation. In
    B. M. Foss (Ed.), Determinants of infant behavior, Vol 4,
    London: Metheun, 1969.

Bailey, P. M., Talbot, A., and Taylor, P. P. A comparison
    of maternal anxiety levels with anxiety levels manifested in
    child dental patients. Journal of Dentistry for Children,
    1973, 40, 277-284.

Berecz, J. M. Phobias of childhood: etiology and treatment.
    Psychological Bulletin, 1968, 70, 694-720.

Bowlby, J. Attachment and Loss, Vol. 2. Separation: Anxiety
    and Anger. New York: Basic, 1973.

Bronfenbrenner, U. The ecology of human development,
Cambridge, Mass: Harvard University Press, 1979.

Cohn, J. R. Three-month old infants' reaction to simulated
maternal depression. Paper presented at the Meeting of
the Society for Research in Child Development, Boston,
1981.

Cummings, E. M. and Beagles-Ross, J. Toward a model of
infant day care: Studies of factors influencing responding
to separation in day care (this volume).

Davidson, S. School phobia as a manifestation of family disturbance: its structure and treatment. Child Psychology
and Psychiatry, 1960, 1, 270-287.

Eisenberg, L. School phobia: a study in the communication
of anxiety. American Journal of Psychiatry, 1958, 114,
712-718.

Field, T., Gewirtz, J. L., Cohen, P., Garcia, R., Greenberg,
R., and Collins, K. Leavetakings and reunions of infants,
toddlers, preschoolers, and their parents. Submitted for
publication, 1983.

Hock, E. Alternative approaches to child rearing and their
effects on the mother-infant relationship. Urbana, IL:
Educational Resources Information Center/Early Childhood
Education, 1976 (ED 122943).

Hock, E., and Clinger, J. B. Infant coping behaviors: Their
assessment and their relationship to maternal attributes.
The Journal of Genetic Psychology, 1981, 138, 231-243.

Hock, E., Gnezda, M. T., and McBride, S. The Measurement
of Maternal Separation Anxiety. Paper presented at the
Meeting of the Society for Research in Child Development,
Detroit, 1983.

Martin-Huff, E. Parental and Contextual Influences on Chil-
drens' Early Adjustment to Kindergarten. Unpublished
Doctoral Dissertation, The Ohio State University, Columbus,
Ohio, 1982.

Medinnus, G. R. The development of a first grade adjustment
    scale. Journal of Experimental Education, 1961, 30 (2),
    243-248.

Murphy, L. B. The problem of defense and the concept of
    coping. In E. J. Anthony and C. Koupernik (Eds.), The
    child in his family: The international yearbook of child
    psychiatry and allied disciplines (Vol 1), New York: Wiley-
    Interscience, 1970.

Murphy, L. B. The widening world of childhood. New York:
    Basic Books, 1962.

Murphy, L. B., and Moriarty, A. E. Vulnerability, coping,
    and growth. New Haven: Yale University Press, 1976.

Nunnally, J. C. Psychometric Theory. New York: McGraw
    Hill, 1978.

Otto, U. The behavior of children when visiting the dentist.
    Svensk Tandlakar-Tidskrift, 1974, 67, 207-222.

Rodriguez, D. T. and Hignett, W. F. Infant day care: How
    very young children adapt. Children Today, 1981, 10,
    10-13.

Rositer, B. A. A developmental guide to starting an infant
    or toddler in day care: Obtaining the benefits while dealing
    with the problems, 1982. (Available from Louise Child Care
    Center, Pittsburgh, PA.)

Rutter, M. Influences from family and school. Paper presented
    at the Meeting of the Society for Research in Child Develop-
    ment, Detroit, MI, 1983.

Schaffer, R. S. Mothering. Cambridge, MA: Harvard Univer-
    sity Press, 1977.

Sorce, J. R., Emde, R. N., and Klinnert, M. Maternal response
    signaling: its effect on the visual cliff behavior of one-year-
    olds. Paper presented at the Meeting of the Society of
    Research in Child Development, Boston, 1981.

Waldfogel, S., Coolidge, J. C., and Hahn, P. B. The develop-
    ment, meaning, and management of school phobia. American
    Journal of Orthopsychiatry, 1957, Vol 27, pp. 754-780.

Waldron, S., Tobin, R., Stone, B., and Shrier, D. School phobia and other childhood neuroses: systematic study of children and their families. American Journal of Psychiatry, 1975, 132, 802-808.

Weinraub, M., and Lewis, M. The determinants of children's responses to separation. Monographs of the Society for Research in Child Development, 1977, 42, (4, Serial No. 172).

Weinraub, M. and Frankel, J. Sex differences in parent-infant interaction during free play, departure, and separation. Child Development, 1977, 48, 1240-1249.

Winer, G. A., A review and analysis of children's fearful behavior in dental settings. Child Development, 1982, 53 (5), 1111-1133.

Yarrow, L. J. The development of focused relationships during infants. In J. Hellmuth (Ed.), Exceptional infant, Vol. 1. Seattle, WA: Special Child Publications, 1967.

Index

attachment, 7, 9-10, 11, 16, 24, 64-65, 66, 68, 99-108, 109, 110-11, 123-28, 133-34, 150-56, 161, 163-64, 165, 171-72, 176, 189; as related to quality of care, 24-25, 110-11, 164, 165; development of, 101-03; Strange Situation (with caregivers), 110-11, 112-13, 124-25, 126, 133-34; Strange Situation (with mothers), 24, 88, 104, 110, 112-13, 114, 122, 124-28, 163-64, 165, 176-92; types of, 7, 15-16, 99-100, 103-04, 122, 125, 128, 172

Bayley Scales of Infant Development, 6

Chicago Study of Child Care and Development, 36-62
cognitive enrichment of day care, 5-6

day care: as contrasted to family day care, 41-43, 59-62, 65-66, 70-73, 83-87, 88-94, 166; as contrasted to nursery schools, 43-46, 47-50, 59; as contrasted to sitter care, 36-37, 38-41, 47-48, 59, 65-66, 70; developmental effects of, 2-3, 23-24, 26-27 (see emotional effects, intellectual effects, linguistic

effects, social effects); dimensions of group size and composition, 18-19, 21, 55-58, 161, 163-64, 165-67, 169-71, 175-76; dimensions of quality of physical environment, 24-26, 37, 57-58, 161, 165; dimensions of caregiver-child ratio, 18-19, 20, 21, 23, 37, 44-45, 55-57, 64, 161; dimensions of care-giver characteristics, 37, 45-46, 57-58, 161; dimensions of caregiver training, 18-19, 61; dimensions of caregiver involvement, 25, 165; dimensions of center size, 20-21, 170; quality of, 8, 16, 21, 26-27, 91-92, 110-11, 161; quality of stability of care, 8, 11, 20, 93, 109, 161, 163-64, 165-67, 169-71, 176; quality of high quality center, 22, 25-26, 111; quality of low quality center, 22, 24, 25-26; personality, 63-64; policy concerning, 2, 16-19, 133, 176, 198-99

emotional effects of day care, 6-11, 15-16, 162 (see also attachment)

father-child relationship: 126, 172

209